Behind the Scenes
at the Local News

BEHIND THE SCENES
AT THE LOCAL NEWS

A PRODUCTION GUIDEBOOK

ROBERT S. GOALD

Focal Press
Boston London

Library of Congress Cataloging-in-Publication Data

Goald, Robert S.
   Behind the scenes at the local news: a production guidebook /
          Robert S. Goald   p.   cm.
   Includes bibliographical references (p.).
   ISBN 0-240-80153-9 (acid-free paper) :
   1. Television broadcasting of news—United States.
2. Television—Production and direction. 3. WJZ–TV (Television station : Baltimore, Md.) I. Title
PN4784.T4G55 1994
070.1'95—dc20

                                        93–44166
                                          CIP

British Library Cataloging-in-Publication Data
A catalogue record for this book is available from the British Libra

Butterworth–Heinemann
313 Washington Street
Newton, MA 02158

10 9 8 7 6 5 4 3 2

Printed in the United States of America

To my parents,

Jean *and* Elmer,

for their love, laughter, and
limitless understanding

and to future television journalists

Contents

Foreword

Television's daily news is the product of a complex and changeable process. Pictures and sounds combine in powerful ways that often provoke and energize viewers. Working in a fiercely competitive system, newscast producers face budget-cutting managers, eager politicians, and a chorus of critics. While journalism and all media have become part of the national debate, television news is the most visible and controversial.

Robert Goald's comprehensive book and companion videotape analyze the production of a major-market newscast, looking at one local station's news from the inside. We follow a reporter and photographer on an unexpectedly timely field assignment. While following along with the producer's script, carefully explained by Professor Goald, the reader and viewer can watch an actual newscast, discovering how each aspect of the production contributes to the program.

In addition to this useful and informative video, Professor Goald has written a unique book that not only comprehensively analyzes local news production, but also thoroughly investigates what local news has become in a world of rapidly changing technology.

As Professor Goald points out, news is no longer the domain of a single department or a handful of veterans who simply work the phones and then write a story. Television journalism is a complex phenomenon that defines and propels a station. By offering an integrated and thorough analysis of one news operation, Professor Goald's study of WJZ-TV, Baltimore, shows where this industry is headed.

—*John Doolittle*
Director of Journalism, School of Communication
The American University

Acknowledgments

Any project of this magnitude requires the support and cooperation of many individuals. The management and staff of WJZ-TV in Baltimore were of immeasurable assistance to me, and graciously gave much of their valuable time to see that every detail in this book was as accurate as possible. I would particularly wish to thank Marcellus Alexander, Gail Bending, Margaret Cronan, Helene King, Denise Koch, Donna Miller, Melissa Sander, and in particular I must single out Richard Seaby, who initially encouraged the project and Guy Raymond, who made it all happen.

At The American University, I would like to thank Dean Sanford J. Unger and Associate Dean Glenn Harnden of the newly independent School of Communication for granting me course release time to complete this book. In addition the support and advice of Dr. John Doolittle was invaluable.

At Focal Press, I am indebted to Phil Sutherland, who saw the merit of this project early on, and to Sharon Falter, whose patience allowed me to complete it.

Thanks and appreciation are also due to Delene Carlee, Harry Fuller, Elizabeth E. Monteleone, Charles Roggero, Megan Snyder, Brandon Thomas, Rob Tregenza, Ph.D., Kim Tudor, Professors David H. Weaver and G. Cleveland Wilhoit.

1

Local Television News: A Current Affair?

Throughout the 60s, and part of the 70s, people who knew local television news were saying, "What a business!" This economic enthusiasm translated into 40 percent operating profits and reaffirmed the old adage that a broadcast license was a license to print money. By the late 70s and into the 80s, broadcast management was saying, "Our business is changing." This belief derived from the explosive growth of new technologies. By the mid-80s, the operant quote became "Our business has changed," and by the late 80s and early 90s, management declared, "Our business has changed and will never be the same." Network television ratings and share had plummeted to record lows due to the fragmentation of the television audience, which included cable, the ubiquitous VCR and, in the near future, the new technologies of fiber optics and direct broadcast satellite (DBS) TV.

Marcellus Alexander, Vice President and General Manager of WJZ-TV in Baltimore, a Group W, Westinghouse operation, while discussing the state of affairs in locals news as we enter the mid-90s, provided us with the current operant philosophy and a new word in the lexicon of local news. "If we are to survive [the new word being *survive*] we must make systemic and fundamental changes in the way that we do business."

Harry Fuller, news director at KPIX-TV in San Francisco (another Group W operation), echoes this belief: "Before 1985, no TV news director ever got in trouble for going over budget. That's no longer true. Why? Business is hurting. Many unions are losing large chunks of their jurisdiction through new contracts and computerized technology. The economics of TV has changed dramatically: money has flowed [away] from networks and their local stations into cable and program syndicators" (personal correspondence).

In the early 1990s the Federal Communications Commission (FCC) predicted in a staff report that most small-market TV stations (those ranked below fiftieth; see Appendix 3) would not turn a profit for the remainder of the decade. Inevitably, then, local television news, like many sectors of the American economy, must not only embrace dramatic change but bring about its own evolution.

Since television is vulnerable to many pressures—economic, social, governmental, and even moral—is local television news free of bias? Is it possible that the kind, or amount, of information presented has been compromised by the permissive, free-market broadcasting philosophy?

Analyst Michael Parenti has made some intriguing observations: "Does ownership of the media translate into control over information? Or are reporters free to write what they want? Reporters themselves offer contradictory testimony on this question. Some say they are independent agents while others complain of control and censorship" (Parenti, 33).

Indeed, media owners and operators place primary political pressure upon the nature of the local news product. Many newspaper owners—Rupert Murdoch and Katherine Graham, for example—call the shots regarding the content and slant of their dailies. Perhaps the most overt and comprehensive illustration of owner control can be found in a memorandum from C. Peter Jorgensen, the publisher of Century Newspapers, Inc., who informed the editors of all his papers that he "did not intend to pay for paper and ink, or staff time or effort, to print news or opinion pieces which in any way might be construed to lend support, comfort, or assistance, or aid to political candidates who are opposed by Republican candidates in the November election" (Jorgensen, 18).

Local station owners also take such stands. Many controlling interests of regional broadcast stations would prefer their operations to project an image that upholds the status quo and steer clear of controversy. Many owners believe that local news should not be a forum for free speech but a marketplace for palatable information—certainly not an arena for patriotic dissent.

Not surprisingly, station owners themselves, regardless of their own opinions, usually pay attention to the opinions of another force in local television: advertisers. You do not bite the hand that feeds you. In smaller designated market areas (DMAs), a town or region may be almost completely supported by a particular industry—shoe factories, assembly plants, breweries. Most local news stations would not present stories damaging to the image of a locality's major economic force. In particular, automobile manufacturers and dealers as well as supermarkets are notoriously hair-triggered to pull ads.

This purely political guideline is not always followed, however. In Baltimore, a local meat-packing company, planning to close its plant and move elsewhere, ignored local government officials, who asked it to negotiate with its employees and keep the plant open. Since the meat company had been a steady source of advertising income for local station Channel 13, the station's sales department implored its news department not to run any stories that might jeopardize revenues from the company. Nevertheless, the news department decided to run stories about the situation, and predictably, the meat company pulled its advertising from the station. Despite this result, in a rare instance of impartiality, the executive news director at Channel 13 admonished the sales department to keep its nose out of the news department's affairs.

In most instances, advertising dollars will influence, to varying degrees, the decisions about what is called news and, more important, what is offered to the public every day.

Some less obvious factors influence the nature of local television news. The television journalist himself or herself helps shape the information the audience receives. Despite their claims of objectivity, many journalists have built-in biases and postures. For example, most journalists come from white-collar, not blue-collar, families, and a large majority are college educated.

During the first three decades of television journalism, the average television journalist was a middle-class, conservative white male. With the advent of affirmative action in the '80s, a sizable population of African Americans have arrived in television journalism—especially in the local news.

In the 1990s, the average television journalist is thirty-three years old. A recent study by Weaver and Wilhoit revealed the racial, religious, and political diversity of television journalists (see the accompanying table) (Weaver and Wilhoit).

Religious Affiliations of Television Journalists	
Protestant	52%
Catholic	36%
Jewish	1%
Other	5%
None	3%
Refused comment	3%
Ethnic Origins of Television Journalists	
All minorities	12.5%
African Americans	6%
Hispanic Americans	4%
Native Americans	1.5%
Asian Americans	1%
Political Leanings of Television Journalists	
Far left	2.2%
Medium left	25.5%
Middle of the road	48.9%
Medium right	17.5%
Far right	5.8%
No comment/Don't know	0.1%

And with the influx of new socioeconomic "types" come perceptual differences about what constitutes local news. All television journalists feel uncomfortable writing or presenting stories that encourage reactions, beliefs, or intellectual conclusions that are diametrically opposed to their own. Investigative reporting—especially the type that can devolve to the level of exposé—quickly becomes an instrument that helps reinforce the station's party line, whatever that line might be.

Above all else, on-air journalists must be totally credible to the audience. They must cultivate and project not only objectivity and sincerity, but also intelligence, wit, and an incisive edge of comprehensive *knowledge* about the subjects discussed and reported. When such qualities are not evident to the audience, the journalist stands on shaky ground. It is, then, very difficult for a newscaster to reveal his or her ignorance of a situation. Parenti comments on this conundrum by saying, "What we sometimes end up with is *authoritative ignorance* as emphatically expressed in remarks like, 'How will this situation end? No one can say for sure.' Or 'Only time will tell.' Or 'That remains to be seen.' (Better translated as, 'I don't know, and if I don't, then no one else does')" (Parenti, 207).

This necessary authority and credibility is intimately connected with an audience's perception of an anchor or reporter. Some viewers may watch local news habitually and come to consider the anchors like family. Although it might seem odd, this sentiment is by and large sincere. Viewers unconsciously want to trust the authority figures represented by anchors and reporters. They want to feel that the local journalists are talking directly to them, and they prefer to believe that the newscast provides them with a chance to share emotions and reactions in a comfortable, nonthreatening atmosphere. Authority is far more acceptable when the TV personalities are perceived as "real" people.

However, according to Harry Fuller: "The old adage that the anchor is a member of the family . . . is not borne out by viewer behavior or market research. Older viewers tend to care more about personality than baby-boomers, African Americans more than Asians, etc. Does anyone think Jennings is Number One solely because of his personality?" (personal correspondence).

Thus the perception of local news has been changing dramatically, along with perceived changes in the marketplace. As mentioned, when during the late '70s and early '80s, local television news became a profit center for many regional stations, general managers and program directors recognized that to compete for ratings (and thus revenues) they had to change their traditional emphases.

The single most obvious trend in local television news is a disturbing and seemingly out-of-control mania for high ratings. The traditional ideals of journalism are being replaced by the zealous greed of capitalism.

In 1986 local news programming at KCBS-TV in Los Angeles was running a weak third in the ratings. CBS, the station's parent company, was concerned that the low ratings might eventually drag Dan Rather's "CBS Evening News" out of first place nationally. Something had to be done. New management arrived on the scene and scrapped almost all the traditional trappings of the local broadcast, including the high-paid anchors. "It's time for a change," said Frank Gardner, KCBS's new general manager. "We have a video-savvy audience watching a news form invented thirty-five years ago. It's got to be more in tune with the California of 1986" (Adler, 70).

The radical format changes and infusion of high-tech graphics were not particularly successful, but KCBS's experience will never dissuade local news directors and program directors from falling prey to the politics of ratings. Rather than showing a decline in the rush to glamorize local news productions, the trends indicate that the glamorization is ever increasing.

Even more bothersome than the instant fix-up, and its obligatory change of sets, anchors, graphics, and opening theme music, is the growing belief that we are entering the age of the subliterate audience, unable to sit still long enough to be informed or enlightened by any of the traditional methods. A 1993 Department of Education survey reported that nearly half of all Americans lacked requisite skills in reading and writing English (Celis, 27). According to the growing philosophy of the local news industry, such audiences are quickly bored, because of the ascendancy of the video culture and the dominating influence of MTV on younger viewers.

Harry Fuller, however, feels that a significant percentage of the modern audience is "post-literate" and doesn't want any more reality. "This is a decade of escape more than the 1950s. These folks are busy, smart, scared of the economy, and can't be fooled. They don't trust me, TV, you, the Congress, or the local car dealer" (personal correspondence).

Pandering to an audience with a short attention span, a lack of interest in things of substance, and a remote control in each hand reveals a medium that lacks respect for its audience. In a recent examination of a Fox local news operation, WSVN-TV in Miami, perhaps the most tabloid-styled station in any major market in the United States, the local station's obvious disdain for the material it presents is clear: " . . . stories are zooming across the screen at a dizzying speed, accompanied by graphics and sound bigger and bolder than anything Miami viewers can find elsewhere. A stalker, a drive-by shooting, the trial of a hit-and-run driver, the confession of a murderer for hire. On and on, the cavalcade of mayhem continues. . . ." (Rohter, H34). Such content, leaning toward the sensational rather than the substantive, appeals to the escapist quality of entertainment programming that the television industry has defended for more than thirty-five years. The tone at WSVN is purposely flamboyant and visually aggressive, according to news director Joel Cheatwood: "[The station] lives by the basic philosophy that news is inherently boring . . . that a faster, glitzier, more upbeat style" is the only way to capture and retain viewers. Cheatwood adds: "We pay as much attention to the esthetics of the broadcast as we do the content" (Rohter, H34).

This kind of programming harbors a basic cynicism that is overtly manipulative. Paul Steinle, director of journalism at the University of Miami, calls WSVN-TV "the worst example of local news I have ever seen in the United States. They do not cover the news. Their entire agenda is set by whatever pictures they can line up."

This kind of local news, operating under the aegis of a network that presumably offers a newsgathering superstructure to supply its affiliates with information, technology, and direction, is dangerously close to a relatively new subspecies of television news aptly termed *tabloid TV*. The eruption of tabloid TV is an embarrassment to everyone involved, but since it is a lucrative business, it is not only tolerated but sometimes imitated. However, tabloid vanguard "A Current Affair" has recently positioned itself in the marketplace in such a way that suggests less lurid and sensationalized programming in the future.

The typical tabloid format features a fashionable host/hostess team, lots of splashy graphics, ten-second teasers, and grainy photos and video of an endless parade of sleaze: drug lords, wife killers, kiddie-porn dealers, insane teenagers, "outed" homosexual celebrities, and tawdry affairs of the ultra-rich. Tabloid TV shows also like to hide under the guise of crusader, saving the unwitting public from the con men and scammers supposedly lurking on every street corner.

	WSVN Miami	WWOR New York	KCBS L.A.	WBBM Chicago	WRC Wash
% of tabloid stories at top of broadcast	74	60	58	51	46
Most consecutive tabloid stories at top of broadcast	22	7	4	5	6
Stories involving murder, shooting, kidnapping, or suicide	28	28	11	15	16
Stories involving disasters, accidents, illness, or product tampering	39	20	19	15	5

From "Tabloid Sensationalism Is Thriving on TV News," Howard Kurtz, *The Washington Post*, July 4, 1993, p. A20.

Nationally syndicated programs such as "Hard Copy" were the first to bring tabloid "news" to television. Before long local news facilities caught the winds of change and trendiness and began producing tabloid segments for their own local news broadcasts. (Preferably, they produced entire thirty-minute shows that could concentrate on the sleazier events in their own DMA.) Incredibly, the tabloid formula has spawned subgenres that concentrate on the activities of criminals as they happen—as seen through the eyes of arresting police officers in local municipalities. Through the miracle of minicams, the audience rides nightly in the backseat of a police cruiser and into the homes and yards of perpetrators. The video is raw, the script nonexistent. Such exploitative TV is low-brow entertainment disguised as journalism, with only a thin veneer of misguided self-importance separating it from the weekly offerings of the World Wrestling Federation.

WWOR-TV, an independent station in Secaucus, New Jersey, serving the New York area, airs a weekly segment called "Case File" that re-creates crimes and contains a voiceover like that of "Dragnet." One recent report reenacted a bank robbery in Queens, New York, with actors and a dramatic score.

As troubling as the advent of tabloid TV might be, there is an even more disturbing trend fueling the politics of local television news: the belief that local news operations should model themselves after tabloid-style newscasts. Frank O'Donnell, former staffer at WTTG-TV, Channel 5 (a station in Washington, D.C., owned by Rupert Murdoch), witnessed such disturbing changes when Kimberly Montour was hired as the news director for Channel 5. Montour was a protégé of Ian Rae, who made a name for himself as executive producer of "A Current Affair." "During my eight years at this station [WTTG-TV], I'd seen the real inside story: the advent of tabloid television and its pervasive influence on both national and local newscasts, boardroom backstabbings and petty power plays, blatant attempts by Murdoch's managers to manipulate the coverage of Clarence Thomas's nomination to the Supreme Court, a fraudulent story about mass murders aimed at selling a movie, and a bogus 'public service' program geared around a 'gimmick' of giving rewards for crime solvers" (O'Donnell, 39). O'Donnell finally left the station because he felt the news was being unceasingly compromised. "We produce a product like American Can Company, only we produce pictures," said O'Donnell.

This sentiment leads to a slight digression about sports coverage in local news. Does its pervasive presence have any connection to advertising demographics? In many cities with professional sports franchises, such as Baltimore and Washington, local news becomes a booster for sports, which happens to rely heavily on TV coverage. Harry Fuller poses an interesting question: "Is it not odd that such a minor field of human endeavor as [professional] sports has become a major part of most news programs? Research shows less than one fourth of the viewers want to watch a sports segment inside the local news. In many places there is no sports at noon, or on the 5:00 p.m. news. Heavy female audiences there. Weather usually scores about 95 percent, with politics, education, crime, health, and economy somewhere over 60 percent" (personal correspondence).

However, some local news strategies are far less desirable than feeding sports scores to a middle-class male audience. Perhaps a greater tragedy is pawning off a product as fact when, in a growing number of cases, it is either an approximation of the truth or a total fabrication.

In 1991 a reporter for KCNC-TV in Denver, Colorado, was convicted of setting up an illegal pit bull fight, during a ratings sweeps period, for a segment entitled "Blood Sport." In Alexandria, Minnesota, a reporter and cameraman for KCCO-TV doing a story on underage drinking brought several cases of beer to a teenagers' party.

A major cause of such setups is the increasingly blurry line, in the minds of TV executives, between news and entertainment. Apparently, television's decision makers perceive few or no differences between news and entertainment—or perhaps they purposely mix the two. Later in this book a staffer at WJZ-TV sincerely refers to the station's product as "infotainment"—a neologism so absurd it smacks of unintended self-parody. The word *infotainment* embodies all that is wrong with trendiness and political correctness, yet the word is gaining acceptance among the very people who should find its coinage the most abhorrent.

Ian Mitroff and Warren Bennis, in their book *The Unreality Industry*, state that the tendency to combine fact and fiction, enrichment and diversion, is helping to establish "pseudoreality." It is a frightening premise: a state of mind and culture in which it is not only difficult to differentiate between truth and falsehood, but also unnecessary because no one really cares anymore. Local television news is only one example of a growing trend toward unreality, say the authors, but it is a high-profile, high-influence medium, and cannot be ignored. They go on to make the following mordant yet unassailable observation: "The supreme irony about TV news is that in the end it fails miserably on two accounts. First, it is not truly informative and therefore is not really news. Second, it is not even good entertainment." Their ultimate conclusion is not as silly as it may seem:

If current trends continue, why shouldn't news take

on the form of a game show? . . . TV justice has already assumed precisely this form in "The People's Court." Once traditional boundaries are no longer sacred and therefore are up for constant experimentation, and even more for commercial exploitation, no proposal, no speculation, on the future of America is too outrageous to be dismissed. On the contrary, in order to capture the current drift of where America is headed, the only valid predictor (guarantor) of America's future may be outrageousness. (Mitroff and Bennis, 17–18)

Another problem arises regarding the faithful presentation of a sequence of events—the actual sequence and pace in which the story's events occurred. In a broadcast story that is almost never more than three or four minutes long, it is impossible to accurately chronicle events that may have occurred over hours, weeks, or years. Instead viewers get a distillation, a compression of events that attempts to relate the feelings and knowledge of those on the scene. But does this really happen?

In almost all cases, no. Videotape editors are routinely instructed to cut out all the boring stuff, the footage that doesn't provide good video. This is tantamount to a distortion of the facts.

Jerry Mander calls this situation in news reportage a "bias towards peaks of content." He feels that since much of what viewers learn about the world is removed from their personal experience, news and information the audience receives from another source (that is, the news industry) becomes the sum total of all the data regarding the forces and elements that affect our lives. That makes news distortions a very serious matter (Mander, 319).

Other writers and analysts have observed this trademark of television journalism. Edward Epstein explains not only the problem, but also why it persists: "Presenting events exactly as they occur does not fit the requisites of television news. But even when coverage presents no insurmountable problems, given the requirement that a network news story have definite order, time and logic, it would be insufficient in most cases to record from beginning to end the natural sequence of events, with all the digressions, confusions and inconsistencies that more often than not constitute reality . . ." (Epstein, 152–53).

Then what do we actually see on television? Epstein feels

that reality is created by the conflux of those who work to broadcast a story—because everyone involved has individual expectations concerning what the story should be—and therefore much of what the audience sees has been shaped, and possibly predetermined, by this complex web of expectations (Epstein, 180).

If the culture at large faces such a future, what might be the future of television in general and television news in particular? Mitchell Stephens, chairman of the Department of Journalism at New York University, believes that television will evolve along with society. Loosely put, this "New TV" will not depend on a rival medium—print, which is basically linear, literal, and interpreted privately at one's own pace—to prepare and largely educate the audience. The television of the future is expected to be "hyper," disjointed, nonverbal (Stephens, G5).

According to Stephens music videos are the major influence on the New TV. They frequently incorporate elements of experimental or avant-garde filmmaking, avoiding the paradigm of classical narrative structure. The self-restrictive length of a three-minute song forces video directors and writers to create impressionistic montage rather than the linear, logical form usually found in print.

Commercials have also been a major contributor to this forced evolution. The thirty- or sixty-second window, through which a large volume of information, enticement, and persuasion must pass, is a tremendous shaper of the medium itself. Again, time is the primary consideration. Advertisers always ask: How fast can we get our ideas across and how many ideas can we cram through the time-window?

Apparently quite a few.

Stephens writes: "Consider . . . a commercial for the Sega video game system. The ad is only 30 seconds long, yet it manages to hurl at the viewer *48 different images* [italics mine] . . . an average of 1 1/2 images per second. . . ." At first glance, one may not believe that any real communication is taking place (especially when there is no traditional narrative accompanying the visuals), yet the spot is cogent enough to allow viewers not only to get the message, but also to recall distinct images from the video blitzkrieg.

Imagining this kind of television as the future norm is both intriguing and quite frightening. How can anything real, anything of substance, be communicated by a series of flashy, brightly colored pictures that may or may not have specific relevance to the subjective viewer? If television news broadcasts take their cues from MTV and commercial spots, the current ten-second sound bites and fifteen-second video cuts will soon seem unbearably long. Once you have raced down the highway at 100 miles per hour, 55 seems ludicrously slow. Future generations of local news audiences may well ask: *How fast can you tell me what I need to know?*

How much of what is happening in daily broadcasting is pushing the limits of the First Amendment? Critics of television news claim that newscasts demonstrate a growing irresponsibility toward presenting the truth, as evidenced not only in tabloid TV but also in the now-famous General Motors truck fires and "Dateline NBC." Critics also claim that many self-proclaimed journalists are too willing to hide behind First Amendment protections rather than clean up their newsgathering techniques.

The long-running debate regarding how much the government should influence broadcast standards always returns to one point: when does control becomes censorship? Traditionally the FCC has had the power to decide who may stay on the air and who will not, who may remain in business and who will lose everything. But since the Reagan years, the FCC's power has been eroded; even enforcement of the time-honored Fairness Doctrine, which provided for equal access time on the airwaves for different viewpoints and opinions, has been relaxed. If those with dissenting points of view no longer have an outlet on the airwaves, the daily news may become more slanted: those who control local news may come to believe that whatever they say or do will be protected under the First Amendment.

Perhaps this trend is evolving into what Stephen Bates, a media scholar at the Annenberg Washington Program of Northwestern University, calls "rubber gloves communication"—it is okay to report or announce *anything* "... as long as you can attribute it to someone else" (quoted in Diamond, 15). The outrageous headlines and doctored photographs of "UFO aliens" in the comical *World Star* and other tabloids may no longer appear only on cheap newspulp. Edwin Diamond writes: "The idea of reality itself will be under pressure. Computer techniques now make it possible to play with photographic images, creating snow, say, in a desert to sell thirst-quenching beer in TV commercials. Soon reality rearrangers may move on to more manipulative ends, such as placing two figures closer together for a 'better'—more compromising—picture" (Diamond, 20).

Local television news is pressured, by a variety of forces, to react, emote, comfort, and change. Cultural mutations in the form of social mores, artistic license, audience perceptions, and changes in national political perspective have all contributed to the changes that are usually reflected in more classically accepted economic influences. In other words, television feels cultural changes in more ways than just the bottom line. While at this writing the industry's pulse is healthy, it is also frenetic and outsized. Some trends diverge widely from the traditional. Having grown up and then "grown young" again through the infusion of new technologies and a new generation of artistic and commercial forms of communication, the news industry will be a major force in its own evolution.

In sum, a word of advice: students drawn to television journalism out of a personal need to serve the public weal should be cautious about their career aspirations. Although television careers have historically been challenging and exciting, remember that good television journalism demands integrity and social responsibility.

Legitimate television news—especially at the local level—can survive the recent bottom-line mentality because of its inherent value to its audience. Local news programming can focus on problems and accomplishments in the microcosms of the city, small town, and neighborhood. It can retain regional attention through its daily routine and help instill a sense of community in all its viewers. Local television news is one of the purest forms of "narrowcasting," and it works because it emphasizes what impinges upon the familiar world of its audience.

The tabloidization of news programming does represent a legitimate threat to good local television journalism. But as long as journalists-in-training understand the need for integrity and responsibility, the danger can be averted. If students truly recognize and appreciate television's crucial role in a democratic nation and in the world, then local electronic journalism will not be compromised.

2

Evolution and Anatomy

EVOLUTION

Today local television news has become so familiar and so much a part of our daily lives, it is difficult to imagine that it began as a five-minute filler.

In the late 1940s and early 1950s, to fulfill the FCC requirement that stations devote part of their programming to matters of public interest, local stations broadcast several minutes of regional reportage every day. These early efforts were Spartan affairs, without the sophisticated sets, on-air personalities, or promos that have become the earmarks of today's local news industry. News material was not gathered by station reporters or "television journalists" (as they were eventually called), but by a far more expedient and inexpensive method: it was pulled off the Associated Press radio wire and hastily read by a studio staffer with a moderately pleasant voice and a modicum of pronunciation skills.

Financial Influences

By the mid-1960s, however, local TV news productions began to change. Economics—or more plainly, *money*—drove local stations to beef up their news teams. Compared to the upward-spiraling costs of other kinds of programming, the price of producing a news show was reasonable, even modest. In addition, if the production proved successful, that is, garnered a sizable audience, the potential for advertising income grew with the news team's popularity. News programming's low costs and high revenues proved attractive enough that local station managers could not afford to ignore the format.

A thirty-minute newscast provides only twenty-two minutes of news: eight minutes are reserved for intros, promos, titles, and primarily commercials, which generate large infusions of cash. But this situation is a double-edged sword. While a high ratio of revenue versus production costs may be achieved, presenting all the newsworthy information within the allotted time is difficult. So during the 1980s most local news productions expanded to hour-long formats in the early evening, coupled with midday programs and the traditional after-prime, late-night broadcasts. This schedule represents a dramatic increase in the amount of time devoted to local news since the days when a single sponsor would back a fifteen-minute package of news, weather, and sports scores.

Harry Fuller of KPIX-TV in San Francisco reveals another aspect of the search for a profitable niche:

> Two time-slots of recent popularity among local stations are 6:00 to 7:00 a.m. and 7:00 to 9:00 a.m. Both are often programmed with news. Another smaller trend is the move toward more 9:00 p.m. or 10:00 p.m. newscasts that air one hour before the network affiliates' late news. In this market, the advent of more news choices at 10:00 p.m. actually increased the number of people watching late news. Most major market newsrooms are fired up and ready to go any time between 6:00 a.m. and midnight. Satellites have also made more live coverage possible. KPIX carried the Waco burnout for two hours live the morning it happened. (personal correspondence)

Affiliate Popularity

Management's interest in local television news productions increased when it discovered that the station leading the ratings in local news also consistently led the ratings in network news and sometimes even entertainment programming. For example, Baltimore's WJZ-TV, Channel 13, has been the ratings champion in local news since 1976. The ABC network news, which follows the local news, is also the ratings leader in the Baltimore market. This phenomenon was acutely demonstrated in the late '60s in Chicago, when the owned-and-operated (O&O) CBS affiliate lost its credibility and its viewers during an extensive housecleaning of on-air commentators; CBS's national ratings in the Chicago area plummeted to fourth—below even the local independent's programming.

A sidelight to affiliate popularity was the growing perception that viewers were attracted to a particular local news show not only by the quality of the information, but also by the likability of the on-air broadcasters. And so, as the '70s wore on, local news "personalities" became commonplace throughout the country.

Competition

In most large metropolitan areas (called *designated market areas* [DMAs] by A. C. Nielsen Media Research rating service; Arbitron, another major rating service, calls such regions *areas of dominant influence* [ADIs]), at least three television stations vie for viewers with their news productions. Many DMAs have at least one or two independent stations (not affiliated with a network) that produce full-blown local news programs. Contrast the expansion of local television journalism to the shrinkage of local print journalism (fewer and fewer major cities have more than *one* major newspaper): clearly, maximizing the viewer appeal of the news is now television's primary consideration.

As local television news productions have grown more elaborate and sophisticated, certain strategies and policies have appeared. While newspapers without intense competitors feel no pressure to dress up their news presentation, increasingly most local television news programs present the news in ways that will attract viewers. We will examine some of the accepted strategies for achieving audience appeal.

While the newspaper business has targeted a relatively well-educated, affluent audience, local television news has done just the opposite. Just as most entertainment programmers have historically aimed prime-time comedies and dramas at relatively uneducated, middle-class wage earners, most local station managers have altered their news programs to appeal to the lowest common denominator.

Technology

During the past two decades, incredible advances in electronics have enabled local news directors to produce shows as slick and high-tech as anything the national networks can offer. When the portable videocamera replaced the traditional "film at eleven," local news could achieve the immediate and oftentimes emotional punch of total intimacy that the live look of tape brings to the screen. The availability of news and information by satellite and the use of mobile equipment uplinked to KU-band relays [see Glossary] have also given local news producers the chance to travel out of the studio to the center of the newsmaking situation. The most direct result of this technological boon is the chance to bring real human drama, *as it is happening,* into viewers' homes each day and evening.

As previously mentioned, the rise of news anchors and broadcast personalities has become familiar in local news programming throughout the nation. Since 1970 in many DMAs, popular news anchors and even meteorologists and sports commentators have been featured in promotional spots for local TV news broadcasts. Depicted as local heroes or celebrities, they are often hyped as "hometown boys or girls" to add appeal and, presumably, credibility—and, it is hoped, viewers. It is an unsettling state of affairs in most cities: audiences are asked to choose a particular local news broadcast based on the personalities of the anchors rather than the quality and integrity of the program. Thus critics and others often analyze the decreasing quality of local news.

The on-the-scene reporter, the television journalist, is the major source of information for a news program. Usually a young man or woman, the reporter races around the DMA with a microphone and a camcorder assistant, covering those events chosen as likely sources of "good copy" or, more important, good video. Unlike many print reporters, the mobile TV reporters generally do not cover an assigned beat; the vast majority of TV journalists lack the expertise that stems from regular reporting on a particular subject. Therefore most TV reporters are unable to conduct an in-depth investigation of an incident. It is not unusual for a TV reporter to cover a story at city hall on Monday and follow up on the death an elephant at the zoo on Tuesday. However, there are some TV "columnists" who air regular features on a wide spectrum of subjects such as health or the law.

Local television reporters find out about newsworthy events from astute news directors, local fire and police scanners, or even the local print media. Again, the lack of real beat reporters makes it more difficult for local television news teams to ferret out stories of substantial depth or go behind the scenes and cultivate relationships with those who may provide unique insights or perspectives on a story.

In addition, the nomadic nature of the television journalist compounds the problem. TV reporters usually begin in small local markets and work up the career ladder by moving to larger and larger metropolitan areas; some eventually ascend to a really big city such as Los Angeles, Chicago, or New York and then get a chance to do national/network broadcasts. As a result, a reporter usually never learns the local territory with any depth of knowledge and familiarity. Also, it is difficult for a reporter to develop trustworthy sources of inside information because before he or she becomes truly comfortable with a region and its influential people, the reporter moves onward and, it is hoped, upward.

Time Constraints

Because TV news tries to offer a sense of immediacy—"the news as it happens!" according to the promos—television journalists must work under much shorter deadlines than print reporters, who usually can take a full day to research, investigate, and finally write a story. Television reporters have only hours or sometimes minutes to get a story ready for airing. In the early days of local news, deadlines were not so immediate because there was usually only one news broadcast, at the end of the day. But as the demand grew for more and more inexpensive local programming, reporters found themselves racing against the clock at noon, six, and eleven (and sometimes four, five, and ten too). As local television news evolves, increased complexity brings new solutions to old problems, but it also ushers in new problems as well.

Video Signature

In the early days of local broadcasts, transmission was in black and white and the monstrously large cameras were forever bound to the studio. Most broadcasts rarely ventured beyond the "talking head." However, as technology improved and getting pictures became easier and faster, the philosophy of what made for good news began to change.

As any graphic design student will tell you, effective graphical presentation of a message is always paramount in the communications business. Even the staid traditionalists, the managing editors of the nation's major newspapers, have realized this simple truth. Over the last decade, most of them have injected new life into their pages by adding color, both by using more colorful photographs and graphics, and by creating bolder design features. Gannett's *USA Today* was the harbinger of this trend. The increased use of visuals in newspapers has influenced the kind of news deemed worthy to present to the public—medical, lifestyle, pop-culture, and other nonevent information.

Television news is even more influenced by visuals. Newsworthy events are routinely rejected as televised stories because they are "video poor" or because on-the-scene interviews do not include enough "sound bites" to capture a viewer's (presumably short) attention. For instance, a story on new local legislation that could profoundly affect all regional citizens may never appear on local channels if no impressive video accompanies the story. These criteria did not prevail in the past, and today's situation shows how improved technology does not necessarily lead to improved product.

TV's prevailing wisdom says that to hook the viewer for the entire broadcast, always start off with the strongest story. Often the strongest video, not the strongest story, airs first. Therefore, on the daily broadcast, the quality of each story's video often dictates the order in which it is shown. But what does *strongest* mean? Most research suggests that viewers watch the news for self-improvement, intellectual enrichment, or to enhance their personal safety. Harry Fuller of KPIX-TV suggests this is why "strong issues 'wear out.' News viewers don't care about gun control or abortion anymore. Those are old issues to everybody except Bob Dole. Viewers have all made up their minds; they've heard it all before. They want to know something that other people don't know yet, or some-thing that will make them healthier, safer, or richer. Most viewers don't watch news to cry or laugh or hate or love. They can rent a home video for that" (personal correspondence).

Features

"Features" and "departments," part of the daily package of news programming, have evolved in number and style. Many local stations, for example, schedule shows about health and preventive medicine, legal aid, consumer issues and prob-lems, financial advice, or even "video classifieds" for sales and employment. For viewers who cannot afford a doctor, nutri-tionist, lawyer, or investment broker, this kind of service can be invaluable.

Changing Philosophies

The recent changes in programming philosophy reflect a trend toward growing independence among local news opera-tions. That is, local stations do not need to rely on their network affiliates for information services, technology, or even a pool of potential employees. With less need for affiliate-provided material and direction, local program managers have increased coverage of local government, especially during elections, when local candidates and incumbents may be interviewed, cross-examined, and held responsible for actions and decisions.

Coverage of events and happenings that appeal to a spe-cific regional interest has also increased—such as certain cul-tural stories that would appeal to specific DMAs with high ethnic or religious concentrations. For example, a story about the Pope may receive more local attention in Boston, with its large Roman Catholic population.

Since the late '60s, the use of freelance media consultants has exploded. Supposed gurus of the industry, the consult-ants are believed to know what will make any news opera-tion successful. Those consultants who have raised the ratings of the majority of their client stations demand and receive enormous fees for performing their magic. Usually they conduct an intensive analysis of a news operation's facilities and then provide a list of suggestions for ultimately improving ratings. As a result, one sees very similar-looking sets, graphics, and anchors on local news stations around the country. Like programmers of prime-time dramas and comedies, who slavishly imitate every successful series, consultants for local news stations tend to lean heavily on a successfulformula.

Local Cable News

Perhaps the most radical change in news programming philosophy has occurred in the cable TV industry. The last few years have seen the inauguration of several local cable news operations. The first such operation appeared in New York when News 12 Long Island was launched by Allbritton Communications. Other local news channels soon followed, including the Orange County News Channel which covers suburban Los Angeles; New England Cable News, based in Newton, Massachusetts; Chicagoland, a Midwest channel launched by the Tribune Company; and the two most high-profile channels, NewsChannel 8 in Washington, D.C. (which also serves the suburban fringe markets in Maryland and Virginia), and New York One News in Manhattan. The hallmark of these cable news stations is the emphasis on *local* news.

Local cable services market themselves as hometown news sources. Unlike traditional TV news coverage in the area, these operations do not limit their news to the traditional TV news hours. Their only analog is Ted Turner's Cable News Network, but with a distinctly local focus. The local cable operations fill a niche by providing stories of intense local and even neighborhood interest: town council elections, zoning board discussions and decisions, high school sports, local personalities, and many other stories found only in weekly neighborhood newspapers.

The local cable channels' basic format is a twenty-four-hour schedule, which means they need to fill more time in a few days than most local commercial stations need to fill in a month. They emphasize local politics: grass-roots interests in neighborhood delegates, town and city council members, political decisions that affect narrow portions of the audience—such as the location of stop signs in a neighborhood or the deployment of school crossing guards.

By 1995 the cable news channels will probably be fed by the fiber-optics networks of local telephone companies. Such technology will allow feedback from the cable audience with two-way converters, so that viewers can immediately register their opinions and even their votes. Ross Perot's concept of the electronic town meeting is approaching reality, and may one day give the reins of democracy back to the people.

Live broadcasts via microwave and satellite relay will give local cable news a unique look and personality. Station operators will be able to create "zone-specific packages" for each area within the cable system. This zone concept has been used by many large metropolitan newspapers: they insert a special section dedicated to small areas within the region.

On New York One, the local cable news channel serving Manhattan's five boroughs, almost everything relies on videotape—including anchor segments and on-the-scene reports. In the field, reporters use consumer-grade electronics gear shooting Hi-8 videotape. Using cameras mounted on tripods, they record the scene, their interview subjects, and themselves. The simplicity of the equipment allows the reporters to concentrate on their job as journalist rather than technician or baggage handler (Calem, F9).

New York viewers witnessed a dramatic example of this technique at work when the World Trade Center was rocked by an explosion on February 26, 1993. New York One was the first station to broadcast video from *inside* the building, after "a reporter slipped a handheld camcorder to a still unidentified emergency services worker, who went inside the center and taped the chaos." The videocassette was rushed outside, fed via microwave to the studio, and aired before the competition could get any video except shots of people with handkerchiefs over their faces staggering about the surrounding streets (Calem, F9).

KPIX's Harry Fuller provided additional insight into the New York One operation. It's not as bare-bones as it appears. "They have a bigger staff for covering Manhattan than I have for 5 million people in an area bigger than Rhode Island. They have a huge budget and will lose money for years. I love what they're doing, but let's not romanticize. They use inexperienced, low-priced kids who will leave as soon as they learn how to do their jobs well" (personal correspondence).

Wayne Lynch, news director at Washington's local News-Channel 8, says he wants the station to have an image of solid dependability, without hype or sensationalism. Prior to coming to NewsChannel 8, Lynch worked in Richmond, Virginia, with Joel Cheatwood, the news director at WSVN in Florida, who has championed the tabloid news format (see Chapter 1). Both news directors learned their television journalism craft in the same environment yet have chosen to take their stations in totally opposite directions.

A major difference between local cable news and other local stations is availability. Local cable stations do not need to bombard the audience with urgent messages to tune in at a specific moment; NewsChannel 8's viewers learn that they can tune in anytime for the information that will have the most direct impact on their lives.

However, local cable news does not necessarily emphasize crime and fear. In fact, news director Lynch (who once worked as the primary crime reporter for WMAR-TV in Baltimore) wants to keep things in perspective at his station. People need to know about the crime in their neighborhood, he says, "but they don't need to have a stake driven into their hearts every night." Citing the local news operation in Manhattan, Lynch praised the decision makers of New York One for not falling prey to the temptation to carry a large slate of crime stories. "They do not process a fast-food diet of news," says Lynch. "Fast-food news, like fast food, may keep you going, but I believe you're better off with a well-rounded diet, whether it's food or news."

The economics of local cable is intriguing. The advertising rates are low, which attracts a wide variety of clients. The on-air anchors are not personalities or stars, because the basic programming philosophy does not demand that viewers be attracted by any one personality. In fact, the trend in local cable news is to present the news directly from the field reporters either live or at least from a taped remote at the scene. Additionally, since there are no grossly overpaid "talents" on staff, the station personnel work together more as a unit without resentment or jealousy. Such corner cutting, rather than decreasing the quality of the programming, actually makes it better.

Some of the concepts pioneered at local cable news stations may predict changes that could affect the entire television news industry in the next century. If the current economy is a blueprint for the future, fewer stations will produce local news by the end of the century. In San Francisco, Harry Fuller has seen just this phenomenon. "Here, both KOFY and KICU [small UHFs] dropped [local] news in the past three years. The Fox station in Reno [Nevada] recently fired their whole news department. A similar thing happened in Salinas [California]. Not enough income to support news."

Under the FCC's Cable Television Regulation Act of 1992, some stations will expand to multiple channels on cable, with only one or two being broadcast channels. In the top fifty markets, new time periods will be established (such as WJZ-TV's entry into the 5:00 p.m. news slot). Fuller further opines that "there are widespread hopes that the FCC will soon allow multiple TV station ownership within a single large market." The predicted 500-channel video system, with an interactive phone hookup and keyboard, may foreshadow a whole range of new services that can deliver local news information to the viewer. Fuller envisions the future as follows:

> There will be a menu of all the stories covered by KPIX and the viewer can select and view whatever he or she wants, in any order, and perhaps in a variety of lengths. The cable conglomerates and phone companies are gearing up for this next phase, and many of the broadcasters will find themselves strictly in the software business—because the over-the-air delivery systems will be obsolete for the middle and upper classes. (personal correspondence)

With the coming new technologies, local news should not try to compete with its national counterparts. As a result many local program managers find themselves in an awkward position. While they strive to inform their citizens about events around the world as well as around the neighborhood, they often have trouble striking a balance. Local newscasts are frequently weakened by management's need to meet the demands of the competition.

A direct consequence of this competitiveness is the redirection of station budgets, paying large amounts of money to star news anchors. If the trend continues there will be less and less money available for the latest technological equipment and newsgathering activities, such as hiring more TV journalists and establishing beats for reporters to develop expertise. Desktop video may someday help accomplish such a change (see Chapter 4).

Perhaps the notion that there is now less money to spend

is more perception than reality. Historically, local television operators have been more profitable than almost all other major industries. Change is indeed inevitable.

ANATOMY AND STRUCTURE

This overview of the organization of local television news will provide a firm foundation for a deeper, more intuitive understanding of the archetypal local news operation. Local TV news is part of a larger system of information gathering, and represents a relationship with many other systems and organizations. There are the obvious connections among networks, flagship stations, and other affiliates, and there are also interdependencies of departments within a local station. Many such relationships and connections define the structure and anatomy of local news.

Until recently, there were three major networks—ABC, NBC, and the venerable CBS. With the success of CNN (on cable television) and the Fox Broadcasting Network, several other major players have come to the news table; the relationship between local stations and their network has changed significantly. It is no longer necessary to be a network affiliate to do well in the ratings. For example, KCAL in Los Angeles, WSVN in Miami, and KTVU in San Francisco are all independent stations with substantial followings. As Harry Fuller observes:

> In fact, only weak stations depend on their network. ABC's national strength is based on their clear understanding that strong O&Os make a strong network. Thus most of their local O&Os are number one in news. CBS is still a network oriented company. Thus its stations and Rather's news are weaker. One measure of a station's news strength—how much ahead of the network news ratings are the 5:00 or 6:00 p.m. local news ratings? Beware of any local news program (like KRON-TV) that does not do better than the network news that precedes or follows it. (personal correspondence)

For many years the typical arrangement in television was for local operators to provide a half hour of regional news, weather, and sports before the network feed of national and international news. But as the concept of local news became more popular, local operations grew more complex and lengthy.

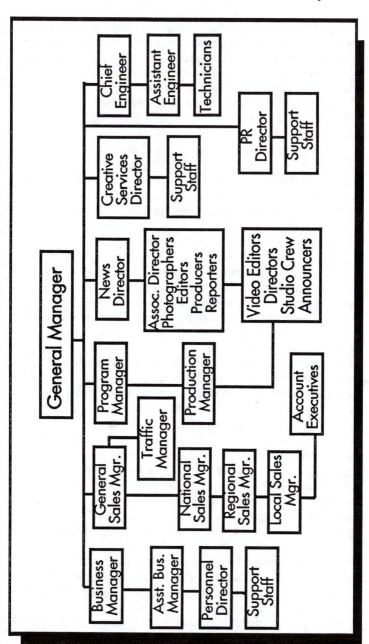

Group ownership is also a noteworthy concept. Most local stations are owned by groups that control more than one broadcast operation. Some groups are quite small, composed of regional business people from rural areas who wish to be involved in communications throughout an area of commercial influence. Other groups are quite large, such as Group W, Metromedia, TVX, Gannett, Scripps-Howard, The New York Times, and Hubbard.

The networks themselves own and operate several affiliates (the O&Os). Until the mid-1980s, the FCC limited the number of stations a group could own to seven, with no more than five VHF channels. Since 1985, under the Reagan administration, the standards have been relaxed to twelve, but no more than 25 percent of U.S. TV households, and it is likely that many groups will expand their holdings.

Group or network ownership has substantial implications for a local news operation. Primarily, it adds an echelon of decision making to the management structure. An independent station may have its own news director or program manager determining the content and quality of the local news; a group-owned station may produce news dictated by a management team or corporate officers with a more regional, or groupwide perspective. In such cases, local news may not be very local. The station in this book's case study, WJZ-TV, owned by Westinghouse, in most instances is not subject to any parent company mandates regarding local news coverage.

What then is the makeup of a truly local station and its news operation? Though it may seem obvious now, once there was a time when people questioned the use and purpose of electronic media (first radio then television). As a new technology in the early decades of the twentieth century, it was extremely important to keep it from becoming an instrument of the government, subject to the extremes of political pressure. Viewed as an extension of the print media, and therefore accorded the same respect for freedom of the press, electronic media developed without government aid or intervention. Radio and television remained privately owned and managed, subject to the pressures of the marketplace, not those of the campaign trails and the halls of legislature. And as the concept of local stations evolved, philosophically as well as physically, a balance of obligations became increasingly clear: television should serve the public welfare and interest but it should also make a profit.

Achieving this balance directly correlates with how well a station is organized and managed. In terms of local news, there is usually a *news department,* with its own news director, who reports directly to the station's general manager. However, no news department operates with complete autonomy, and it must work closely with the other departments in a well-run local broadcast facility.

The *business department* is a centralized division of the station facility. It works closely with all the department heads, and with the general manager, to supervise the income and cost of operations. This department supervises personnel and assists in hiring and firing, and in negotiating contracts with the various unions that represent the staff; performs all general business accounting operations; and advises the general manager on the effects of all spending and financial decisions. The department is also responsible for the administration of retirement policies, insurance programs, and pension funds. The business department also serves as a watchdog for revenues from the various advertising agencies that represent the sponsors, keeps tabs on the credit of the station's customers, and is responsible for the analysis of all financial information relative to the operation of the station not only on a daily basis, but also for the entire year. To help plan for the station's future, the business department must be keenly aware of the general economic climate throughout the nation, particularly in the region that defines the DMA (which is responsible for the majority of a station's revenue) and be able to act quickly on that awareness and knowledge. Perhaps the most significant responsibility of this department is the annual compilation of the station's financial profile—the annual report. Since the fourth quarter is historically the busiest part of the broadcast year in terms of advertising revenues, the business department must be able to analyze and present the largest bulk of the financial information in an efficient and timely fashion. If the station is part of a larger broadcast group or a corporation, the business manager is responsible for supplying the CEOs of the group with corporate-level financial data.

The *sales department* is an important arm of any efficient local station. Account executives are responsible for bringing in revenues through advertising, which allows a station to continue and grow as a business. Sales personnel are often some of the highest-paid station employees, a reflection of their worth to the entire operation, and sales department managers frequently become general managers. The economic clout of the sales department should be obvious, but its operations do not normally influence the operation of the local news department. In most cases, sales and news coexist without pressure or tension. *Traffic,* found in all local stations, is usually a division of the sales department. This division determines where and how often news department spots will air. Scheduling and balancing various types of programming have become an important juggling act at all stations; the insertions of all tapes are normally handled by a preprogrammed computer. Market research and psychological profiling now dictate when the audience is most receptive to commercials, information, and entertainment. Account executives are kept apprised of all the most recent demographic and psychographic data that define and clarify what programming is scheduled to the best advantage. It is the responsibility of the traffic department to see that the schedules are kept and optimized.

The *creative services department* has an important function at the local station—to "sell" the station's programming to its potential audience. Local news is one of the prime clients for creative services because all advertising sold during its broadcast window need not be shared with network godfathers. Therefore, promotions geared to generating interest and appeal for a station's local news package usually emphasize credibility, competence, and the on-air personalities. In recent years features and magazine formats, special inserts in the traditional news, have provided a new area of promotional hype. The feature reporters and magazine-format hosts are often high-profile subjects ripe for promotion. Critics of local news often target feature reporters and their segments because they pander to the the audience. In other words, promoting feature reporters and fluffy magazine segments ensures that the audience is being deprived of more serious issues.

This problem is never more evident than during "sweeps weeks," when the Nielsen Company intensifies its fact-gathering operations to determine who is watching what. The data collected from such polls in turn determine the all-important ratings and demographics of every program on television. And it is demographics that suggest the value of advertising on any particular network or program. Advertisers do not buy air time based on household ratings; they rely on the more relevant demographic information now available. The Nielsen process is a continuing one, but during sweeps weeks (which occur in February, May, and November) the effort to analyze audience preferences becomes a high-energy endeavor. By employing sophisticated electronic samplers and satellite telemetry, Nielsen gives broadcasters feedback literally overnight. Thus during sweeps weeks, every broadcaster in the nation programs material that it believes will attract the largest number of viewers. As may be expected, during sweeps weeks, program and news directors of local television news tend to offer a disproportionate number of stories and features highlighting sex and violence. It becomes the job of the creative services department to use such sensationalized programming in their ads and come-ons. Although other departments should not have decision-making power over news programming, suggestions from the creative services director usually garner more than casual interest from management.

All of the above departments interact or coexist with the news department, but none has the impact of the *programming department* and its manager. Although audiences may not realize the importance of "lead-ins" and "lead-outs," programming departments are very aware that local news ratings are highly affected by the ratings of programs before and after them. Program managers are not as concerned with the success or failure of any single program item, such as the local news, as much as they are with the fate of the station's entire schedule.

Local news should never be perceived as an isolated entity, a stepchild, or a black sheep, in a family of more entertaining members. It is therefore important that program managers attempt to create an environment that makes the local news segments as organically integrated into the schedule as possible. This philosophy is not geared to the audience members who specifically tune in to get the news, but for the "inadvertent audience," who are watching because their entertainment programming has just ended and they have yet to change the channel.

Finally, another department with a high degree of interaction with the newsroom is *engineering*. While the last decade's explosion of accessible technology has allowed anchors, reporters, and photographers to perform some of their own technical work, there is still a great need for a trained engineering staff to troubleshoot or solve special problems. As dependence upon technology such as mobile vans, satellite relay antennae, video camcorders, and on-the-fly videotape editing increases, so does the reliance on technicians and engineers who must stand by to correct inevitable errors, accidents, and unforeseen complications.

There are many advantages to increased reliance on new technology. For instance, the lighting on local news sets has greatly improved. In the earlier days of live studio broadcasting, the cameras were not very sensitive to low levels of light. Sets were ablaze with lighting rigs and everyone on camera was usually perspiring heavily. Today, the low-light sensitivity of state-of-the-art cameras allows sets to be much cooler, and anchors enjoy soft, more aesthetic lighting arrangements.

Any discussion of television news anatomy and/or structure would be less than complete without at least a mention of the industry's current salary structure and a look at the state of affairs for women and minorities.

The table on page 33 lists the average salaries for various positions at local television stations throughout the country. Variance is often determined by the size of the market (Stone,"New Salaries Stand Still," 15).

The past ten years have seen dramatic changes in the numbers of minorities and women working in television news. This trend does not appear to be slowing. In the table on page 34, one can readily see the high percentages of minorities and women on news staffs (Stone, "Little Change for Minorities and Women," 26).

It is clear, then, that the evolution of local news programming as a mainstay of regional broadcasting was complex. Since its humble beginnings, local television news has been influenced by political, social, and economic factors, and affected by the various components of its production and organizational environment. Because television is a high-profile commercial and entertainment medium, national and local television news programming has reflected these realities. The complex relationships engendered during the formation of local news departments provide broadcasters with an interest-

	Typical ENG Cam.	Typical Producer	Exec. Producer	Typical Reporter	Typical Anchor	High Anchor	Assign. Editor	Asst. ND	News Director	N
ADI 1-25	$35,285	$36,500	$57,750	$47,250	$120,835	$194,520	$37,250	$73,750	$92,500	63
Net Affils.	$38,500	$39,915	$64,285	$55,500	$149,585	$263,750	$39,875	$81,430	$107,500	39
Independents	$29,375	$28,750	$42,500	$31,250	$55,000	$62,500	$32,750	$56,500	$52,915	24
ADI 26-50	$24,575	$28,500	$41,565	$30,615	$70,810	$118,335	$34,000	$50,310	$73,250	51
ADI 51-100	$18,475	$21,250	$32,375	$20,500	$39,715	$58,250	$28,035	$35,165	$51,470	106
ADI 101-150	$15,675	$17,800	$21,875	$16,900	$27,450	$35,400	$21,875	$27,875	$37,475	93
ADI 151-210	$13,055	$14,930	$19,500	$13,845	$19,800	$26,625	$17,875	$24,375	$30,080	61
Staff 0-10	$14,935	$16,500	$19,375	$15,140	$18,685	$25,375	$18,250	$18,500	$29,520	55
Staff 11-20	$14,450	$17,160	$21,250	$15,970	$23,950	$32,250	$19,305	$23,500	$36,375	112
Staff 21-35	$18,345	$21,160	$30,350	$21,060	$40,400	$60,125	$27,800	$35,575	$50,460	106
Staff 36-180	$28,025	$30,750	$49,090	$37,550	$80,415	$152,000	$35,130	$57,500	$85,165	107
East	$21,350	$24,750	$39,000	$22,750	$36,250	$70,000	$29,150	$66,250	$50,810	52
South	$17,260	$20,750	$33,500	$19,750	$37,625	$53,625	$27,000	$35,150	$49,835	126
Midwest	$18,750	$22,035	$34,800	$19,360	$35,375	$48,250	$28,200	$44,875	$44,250	112
West	$18,750	$23,700	$40,750	$20,940	$34,750	$47,500	$28,500	$42,500	$44,335	91

	N	News Staffs with Women		Women per News Staff		Female % of Work Force	Staffs with Minorities		Minority Members of News Staff		Minority % of Work Force
		in News	as NDs	Median	Mean		in News	as NDs	Median	Mean	
Television	403	97.3%	16.8%	8.02	10.54	33.7%	83.8%	8.6%	3.00	5.45	17.4%
Network	342	98.8%	14.8%	8.93	11.36	33.7%	83.9%	6.4%	3.03	5.38	16.0%
Independent	57	87.5%	28.8%	3.33	5.84	33.7%	83.7%	30.3%	3.12	6.12	35.3%
ADI 1-25	65	96.8%	20.0%	20.33	20.38	33.9%	94.0%	19.7%	11.67	13.55	22.5%
Network	36	97.1%	17.5%	27.75	30.09	34.1%	97.4%	12.8%	16.50	18.37	20.8%
Independent	29	92.9%	23.3%	5.33	8.25	32.8%	69.0%	29.6%	5.50	7.24	28.8%
ADI 26-50	50	96.0%	12.2%	14.67	13.67	32.7%	93.9%	4.0%	7.00	6.88	16.4%
ADI 51-100	127	97.6%	13.1%	9.64	9.50	32.4%	89.6%	7.9%	2.93	4.23	14.4%
ADI 101-150	94	96.8%	17.0%	6.02	6.86	34.1%	78.5%	9.6%	2.50	2.77	13.8%
ADI 151-208	60	98.3%	21.7%	4.70	5.92	36.8%	61.7%	5.2%	1.08	1.72	10.7%
Radio	274	58.9%	29.1%	.98	.86	29.4%	18.3%	8.9%	.11	.34	11.6%
Major Markets	29	82.8%	51.7%	1.18	2.48	36.5%	41.4%	17.9%	.88	1.24	18.3%
Large Markets	53	60.4%	30.8%	.75	1.13	35.9%	26.9%	14.0%	.20	.48	15.2%
Medium Markets	95	37.9%	22.1%	.30	.48	21.5%	17.9%	8.4%	.12	.22	9.8%
Small Markets	94	44.7%	28.7%	.40	.63	27.2%	7.5%	4.3%	.05	.11	4.7%

ing mix of freedoms and constraints. A new brand of almost-instant journalism and an opportunity to present images of emotional impact to an unprecedented number of people are tempered by a forced sensitivity to the requirements of the economic arena.

This complex organization has been further skewed by the perception among some news directors, programming managers, and promotions executives that local news broadcasts—at least on some level—must be presented as entertainment. This perception gained currency in the early '60s and has continued to be debated ever since.

In the following chapters, we will examine local television news around the nation. We will discover the prevailing principles and political considerations, and learn how local television news is produced—technologically and philosophically. A case study of a news operation in a large DMA will provide us with the means to dissect a typical broadcast day.

3

The Principles of Local News

Certain principles of newsgathering form the bedrock of any local broadcast operation; they define the content, quality, and appeal of any newscast, and are vital to the integrity of programming and the mission of all members of the organization. In this chapter we will examine in some detail not only what these principles are, but also how they became such primary shapers of what we perceive as local television news.

RESPONSIBILITY

Perhaps one of the most enduring ideals in local news broadcasting is responsibility. Television journalists believe in objectivity, which may indeed help explain why they insist on their complete autonomy. Such a major responsibility—a freedom, if you will—allows journalists to ask anyone anything under the guise of locating sources, who will supposedly reveal unfiltered and unbiased information. The problem with such autonomy should be self-evident: the audience is asked to believe whatever it is told.

Another problem is the lack of understanding of the medium's power to convince millions of people to think a certain way or believe a presumed fact. This connects with the issue of locating sources. William A. Henry III, in "News as Entertainment: The Search for Dramatic Unity," reports instances in which TV journalists' so-called sources gave information that the sources themselves learned from a TV news report. Such absurd occurrences resemble a mirror reflecting itself, or the conundrum of the chicken and the egg. Too many people who work in television, by being so close to the operation, forget the power of the instrument they wield.

Henry writes:

> . . . the heaviest burden on a TV reporter [is] the persuasive power of his own medium. Television is made by people obsessed with objectivity but biased towards the mainstream. Its stories are largely limited to the new and the obvious. It seeks to fulfill psychic needs of the audience and yields to dramaturgical needs of the reporter. It avoids moral commitment, yet presents itself as an avenging angel. It compromises its detachments with boosterism. It is edited and purposeful. But while print is gray and abstract, TV looks and sounds like spontaneous life.

Henry makes a trenchant observation about where a broadcast facility's responsibilities should lie. Precisely this aspect of television news, especially the local variety (which often promotes itself to viewers as "on your side," "your friend in need"), requires recognition and emphasis. To be a responsible news director or anchor or journalist, one must carefully verify all information and then use caution in disseminating it.

Indeed, there are legal, as well as moral and ethical, implications to getting the facts straight. A local news operation is under a powerful microscope in its community or region. Anything the facility releases is immediately subject to scrutiny, some of it biased. Care must be exercised in not only what is told in a particular story, but also how that story is told. More than one network's legal department has circulated memoranda to its affiliates regarding words known in the industry as red flags or, more to the point, dangerous. The following short list shows some examples; the complete list is much longer:

atheist
blackmail

bribery
communist
crippled
fascist
fraud
illegitimate
incompetent
Negro
Oriental
suicide
swindle

The message is clear: be careful what you say. Almost anything, however innocuous it may sound, is most assuredly going to be offensive to someone. Even a segment in the video that accompanies this book was red-flagged by station management, to change the word *boy* to *young man* when referring to an African-American youth about twelve years old. Granted, social usage and topical parlance change from decade to decade, and what may now be a fashionable or acceptable term or phrase may someday be libelous. We have entered the era of political correctness, and as a result the reporting of all kinds of information will be further constrained.

It follows, then, that one of the most responsible things a television journalist can do is to exclude conscious values from his or her material. Such conduct is believed to be a practical, effective defense against critics who call for self-censorship by local stations or, better yet, a chance to censor the news themselves.

OBJECTIVITY

The word that appears endlessly in almost all discussion of television journalism is objectivity. Everyone claims to practice it, and some individuals and stations actually achieve it. Objective reporters, news directors, and even anchors/personalities are the ones who keep broadcasts free of their own personal biases. (Two local broadcasters are freed from this dictum: the sportscaster and the meteorologist. The former is expected to be a "homer," a vociferous supporter of all local teams; the latter should be sensitive to the needs of local citizens and is encouraged to describe conditions in subjective terms such as *wonderful, nice,* or *terrible.*)

Objectivity also means that news stories are chosen without regard to whom the content of the story may hurt or benefit. Thus the blade of objectivity cuts both ways. While it is essentially impossible always to present completely inoffensive material, one should not confuse that fact with the idea of impartial, objective broadcasting. TV journalists want us to believe that they are trying to be fair; perhaps given the volatile nature of humans, that is all we can hope for. In other words, it is difficult to remain objective in a social arena where everything is always changing.

How can a journalist even reach an evaluative conclusion about a story he or she is presenting to the public? Because many local reporters become familiar faces or personalities to their viewers, an audience may expect or unconsciously demand that their journalists react in some way to their subject matter. Hence the phrase subjective reactions was coined, for when reporting, say, a local tragedy requires an emotional response from the journalist. Such a display humanizes the entire event and removes the question of a priori judgment or bias.

Indeed, the very nature of local news and its rigid daily schedule promote detachment. TV journalists move so rapidly from assignment to assignment that they normally have no time to invest personally in any one story. When no real attachment to the material is established, objectivity is easy. Assignment and story editors, by the nature of their position, rarely leave their office, which also promotes detachment.

It might be argued that this posture of objectivity can sometimes cause as much harm as good. For example, during the federal trial in California concerning the violation of Rodney King's civil rights, the question was often raised about the multitude of newscasts that, before the verdict in the state trial and the ensuing riots, depicted preparations for lawlessness. Could such reporting actually create a self-fulfilling prophecy? How much information about potential rioting and looting should be included in the local news if it might promote the idea of breaking the law? Similarly, sociologists and forensic investigators have often discussed the phenomenon of copycat criminals, who are inspired by the objective reporting of sensationalistic crimes.

NEWSWORTHINESS

Most principles of local news spark no controversies. Newsworthiness is one of the most universal principles because it encompasses some of the most important notions in television journalism. A story's newsworthiness is measured by the power of its content. Generally considered the major criterion for selecting the lead story in any broadcast, newsworthiness should also play a central role in deciding the place and relevance of all stories. What concepts determine newsworthiness? *Importance, interest, controversy, the unusual, timeliness, proximity, shock value, possible future impact,* and *titillation.* A short discussion of each concept should flesh out and adequately define this important principle. Two additional considerations in terms of newsworthiness not discussed below are *celebrity-interest* (what stars are featured) and *the competition* (what competitors in TV, as well as radio and print, are planning to run).

Importance. An indicator of an event's significance and the size of its effect on the community, the concept of importance also assumes that the story will be unfettered by rumor, limited to local interest but not parochial, and not ultimately trendy or simply bizarre.

Interest. A key criterion, interest is not always intimately associated with importance. Why? Because the audience is not always interested in what may be very important concerning their safety or welfare. People know that vitamins are good for them, but they would prefer to take them in foods that also taste good. Stories with strong interest value may have weak substance, such as the mayor's wife's taste in fashions or films. But in this case, the content does not diminish the newsworthiness.

Controversy. Any novelist or playwright will tell you that a good piece of fiction has plenty of dramatic conflict. A good measurement of a story's worth must include its tension-producing value, the controversy that most audiences enjoy watching. Harry Fuller of KPIX-TV in San Francisco cautions that "controversy is not a permanent value. It has a half-life as surely as does radium. It is a fact of life that most viewers have had a brief period of concern with most things. . . . When was the last time you heard a serious argument about men with long hair?" (personal correspondence)

However, in earlier decades, before local television news became a popular, revenue-attracting operation, the newsworthiness of a story was not always a primary consideration. William A. Henry III recalls that in the late 1970s,

> Local news was often a freak show. The most esteemed station in Boston once began its main newscast with five consecutive fire stories. The anchor on another network-affiliated Boston station referred to Teng Hsiao-Ping twice as "Mr. Ping." San Francisco's most popular station began one newscast that I saw with a teaser about "what X-rays showed in Adolph Hitler's head." Then it cut to an interview with its own technicians, out on strike. Then it cut to footage of a tornado a thousand miles away that had injured no one but had demolished a root-beer stand. Such trivia are the rule, not the exception.

The Unusual. A good journeyman's definition of *news* is "something out of the ordinary." So goes the classic (perhaps hackneyed) "dog bites man" aphorism that originated in the print medium and continues to reign in television journalism. In their never-ending search for the unusual, broadcasters—especially in local markets—are often criticized for putting too much emphasis on bizarre segments, such as features on winners of hog-calling contests; the strangest costumes at a local *Star Trek* convention; or the wacky, useless devices of a local eccentric inventor. Such stories may be amusing, even entertaining, but often they are unimaginative, tiresome, and demeaning.

Similarly, the quest for the unusual can often produce negative content, perceived as depressing, destructive, or pandering to low-brow sensibilities. Again this is a frequent complaint among critics and analysts of local television news. No longer William Henry's "freak show," local television news has shed most of that image by placing less importance on finding something weird for every program.

Timeliness. This criterion is self-evident. In a medium of such total immediacy, television news is expected to be up to the minute. With local news operations appearing at least three, and sometimes four, times each day, audiences have come to expect updates on stories that aired only hours previously. The old newspaper axiom about news being like food—it spoils after it's been out for a while—is even truer about the dynamics of the phosphor screen.

Proximity. In local news, proximity is practically a given. Each potential story is considered based on its relationship to the broadcaster's DMA. However, a story does not necessarily have to occur within the geographic region of the broadcast facility. Many events that happen around the globe nonetheless directly influence affairs in a small region. If, for instance, a European government cancels the purchase of computer components manufactured locally, the story has obvious impact on the local economy. One major caveat: beware of over-emphasizing the regional-interest story. There is a fine line between loyalty to the community and provincialism.

Shock Value. Not necessarily something scary or disturbing, shock value refers to the surprising or unexpected. Stories with familiar elements (causes, locales, or consequences) are not as inherently interesting as stories with elements not normally found together. For example, the story of a mother killed in an automobile accident does not have the shock value of a story about a mother killed by her ten-year-old daughter.

Possible Future Impact. One aspect of newsworthiness may be less recognizable to the average viewer: if a story's potential impact on the future is not evident, it may not make the newscast. In fact many stories go unreported for just this reason. Unless the material contains its own predictive element—for example, the reporter explaining what will happen if the situation persists—the implications for the future may not be apparent to the viewer. The shrewd reporter or producer can see the consequences of every potential story that crosses his or her desk.

Titillation. The concept of titillation is almost always used to describe stories that feature sex and tend to be broadcast during the sweeps weeks. A wealth of material is always available to fulfill a station's need for titillating stories—from swimsuit fashions to local censorship against video rental shops to X-rated computer software.

VARIETY
Since a large portion of the viewing audience tends to stay with the same station for all of its news and information, news and programming directors must present a variety of material from hour to hour. Using microwave relays and satellite tech-

nology, stations can feed breaking news into successive broadcasts around the clock often enough to always guarantee a fresh package.

On a slow news day it may be necessary to reshuffle stories that are only moderately newsworthy, dropping some items because they were aired during the last broadcast. Only major stories with wide-reaching impact should be exempt from the variety principle.

Like the proverbial tree falling in the forest with no one to hear its sound, a news broadcast does not really exist without its audience. Therefore, viewer retention is a prime directive, and variety in programming is essential.

TIMING

Newspapers have traditionally pledged to give their readers "all the news that's fit to print," but television news programs have always provided their audience with all the news that *fits*. Period. There is no room for negotiation.

A broadcast is a window in time, and everything appearing in that window must be circumscribed by the hour or half-hour format. Time, then, is truly of the essence. When a story is written, it is timed out to see how long it will take to read on the air. In order to map out the show, every scripted story has its own time signature—down to the second—along with the running times of videotape insertions.

Experienced television journalists time themselves by adding up the number of lines of their copy, and carrying a stopwatch at work. They can calculate almost to the second how much time is required to deliver a story. So measured is their rhythm, pacing, and oral delivery that the real veterans know how many seconds they will need to read a line of copy. In general, a polished, professional reader allows a maximum of three words per second. The penalty, as declared by the show's producer, for misjudging a story's timing is "death": the story will never be aired. If the journalist must rush through the final sentences or, worse, cut them altogether, the message is compromised.

Timing also varies with the quality, content, and ranking of a particular story; a story's position in the newscast can be influenced by its length. If there is time for only a thirty-second story until a commercial break, a longer but more newsworthy story may have to be postponed until after the break, thus appearing less important than it may be. Harry Fuller notes that "a well-produced newscast will be like a strong piece of classical music . . . slow, fast, solemn, light-hearted, heavy, cheerful, some of the expected, and some surprises."

VISUALS

Images make television news a distinctive medium. In its early years local TV news suffered from unimaginative sets, dependence on quickly processed film, and still photographs or maps. Through the decades, improvements in technology, interior design, and lighting have all helped create a more punchy visual package.

Perhaps the most familiar element is the flat-lit medium close-up: the shot frames the head, shoulders, and chest of the journalist or anchor seated at a desk. If the person was wearing nothing below the waist, the audience would never know it. The standard image is uninteresting and unimaginative, yet it might be necessary for several possible reasons: if there is no video to support an out-of-town story; or if producers are afraid to distract viewers from the verbal message; if a person-ality is featured in the visual programming package.

Graphics are also a major element of visuals, used to accent, enhance, or illuminate a story. Although graphics have historically been simple still images, digital video technology can now incorporate a picture within a larger picture, such as a box beside a talking head. No more dull face-in-a-frame presentation. The still images inserted in the effects box can be photographs, artist's drawings, charts, or logos. Graphics also add style to a broadcast and can help distinguish a local station from its hometown competitors. Major-market players have dedicated graphics generators such as the Paint Box to impart a unique look to each news broadcast, making it more memo-rable or appealing.

The function of the *super* (short for *superimpose*) is similar to that of a general graphic, but supers always depict words. Long-time broadcast veterans sometimes call supers *lower thirds*, for the part of the screen where they usually appear. Even though the audience absorbs most of the story by listen-ing to (as opposed to reading) a series of words, superimposing key words, titles, or phrases over the primary images can very effectively reinforce the main message. The super is also useful because it saves time—as we have seen, a very important factor. Commentators need not identify themselves and journalists need not introduce interviewees. In the broadcast industry, Chyron is the most ubiquitous dedicated character generator (video electronic typewriter) used to produce the insert-key effect.

Other visual elements include the chromakey and Ultimatte, similar to the special-effects "blue screens" used in movies. When the weatherman stands in front of a regional map or perhaps a hurricane-lashed shoreline, the chromakey is used. While their effects can be dramatic and powerful, overuse can quickly lead to cliché. On the other hand, computer-generated art created as needed by an in-house artist guarantees that every image is fresh, used only once, and never seen again. Another advantage of computer-generated art is its capacity for animation when movement is required for further emphasis. Such images follow the principle of visuals: giving the audience the most visually exciting and memorable information in the most efficient manner possible.

TELLING THE STORY

Perhaps the most basic, yet most important, principle is telling the story right. Indeed, if a station stages its broadcast by following all the abovementioned principles and fails to communicate the intended information, then it has not told the story.

The key to telling the story in local news broadcasting begins with the understanding that a story must be written for presentation over the air. With printed material a reader usually can reread or review any section at his or her own pace to absorb complex information such as statistics, tables, or a list of facts. But a broadcast story has no room for review; the audience gets only one chance to take in the information.

Therefore, the first rule in telling the story is to avoid complex sentences—present only one fact per sentence. Second, each sentence should be fairly concise and to the point. A viewer seeking information will not appreciate the beauty of literary prose, and will usually have trouble following it. Third, the story and its facts should not be chronicled like the items on a grocery list, but should be delivered in a conversational style. Anyone who has attended a public speaking engagement knows how easy it is to tune out a speaker who *reads* to the audience instead of *talks* to them. If viewers feel that they are sharing a conversation, they are far more attentive, relaxed, and therefore receptive to new information. The last major aspect of telling the story is word choice. Many newspaper veterans claim that the average person has a working vocabulary—that is, a group of words he or she uses on a regular basis—of less than 300. So the television journalist should be careful to avoid esoteric or long words. The writer should also avoid subtle, nuanced, or obscure words. The same holds true for euphemisms. Harry Fuller was surprised that his own newsroom ceased using the term *ethnic cleansing* long before it disappeared from the networks or even *The New York Times*. "It seemed clear to me that the phrase covered up what was really going on and didn't deliver a clear description to the viewer. In this case, conversational description of the killing, burning, and rapes was a far better service to viewers than to use the more obscure Vietnam-era style phrases coming out of Yugoslavia" (personal correspondence).

Also, words that are indigenous to a particular social group or profession, such as slang or argot, should not be used unless one is explaining their meaning or usage. Foreign words or phrases, even those accepted into English, only confuse, intimidate, and ultimately discourage audiences who do not understand or relate to them. In other words, eschew obfuscation and the *juste mot*.

4

Technology: Exploring the Technical Side of Local News

Over the last twenty-five years, multiple generations of diverse and seemingly unrelated technologies have evolved. Terrestrial microwave systems developed into satellite transmission, and Quad videotape was replaced by 1-inch Type C and 3/4-inch U-matic. The list of technologies that have contributed to the vast array of changes in television production and newsgathering is seemingly endless: Betacam and Betacam SP, the format of choice in the early 1990s; time-base correctors; camcorders; innovative small-tape formats such SVHS and Hi-8; digital video processing; multichannel television sound; robotics; dedicated graphics workstations; flying spot scanners for film-to-tape conversions; and, most of all, computers. Looming on the horizon, coming in the late '90s or early twenty-first century, are high-definition television, direct broadcast satellite, and digital component video.

All technological changes have not uniformly increased news quality or station revenues. As television technology grows ever more sophisticated, it becomes increasingly challenging to train and employ the personnel necessary to operate and maintain it.

Expenditures for technology are part of the broadcast industry; the fiscal responsibility for capital equipment has become the province of the chief engineer and the comptroller. A certain amount and quality of acceptable equipment and technology are necessary to keep a station on the air. Management must make the financial commitment to maintain that minimum level of acceptability, or the station will not survive. Every consideration and strategy concerned with technology must originate from one basic tenet: all equipment will eventually fail or become obsolete.

Every chief engineer knows this inevitability. There are several ways to manage the demands of broadcast industry budgets and technology: purchase and stock replacement parts and equipment before they fail; hedge all bets by acquiring parts as close as possible to expected lifetimes of all material; or replace things only after they have totally broken down. The last alternative is obviously not the stratagem of choice. No professional engineer wants to run the operation close to the edge, but shrinking station revenues caused by additional competition are forcing many to do so.

Gathering and producing the news involves many technologies that were largely unknown a quarter century ago. We will examine some of the most important innovations in the next few sections.

VIDEO RECORDING AND TRANSMISSION

In the mid-1960s, film fell out of favor, and videotape, which can be played back immediately and is easy to edit, revolutionized the news business. Although videotape formats have changed and improved, videotape itself remains the primary acquisition medium in the '90s because it is cost-effective.

The first videotape format, developed in the late '50s, was Quadruplex (Quad for short), a transverse 2-inch format on large, heavy reels that ran on a 1,300-pound machine as big and noisy as a washing machine. Quad was the best format available until 1978, when it was replaced by a more economical recording technology called helical scan. In this tape process, video heads move across the tape surface at an acute angle

1,800 times per minute, resulting in the same writing speed as Quad with a lot less tape. While helical scan tape comes in tape widths ranging from 1/4-inch to 2-inch, the 1-inch format (called Type C)(III [12:07]) was embraced by the industry. This format was the first to allow acceptable playback of images in still frame, slow motion, or accelerated motion. Additionally, Type C decks were less expensive than Quad decks, and Type C raw tape was cheaper too. With Type C, for the first time, limited portable electronic newsgathering (ENG) field acquisition was possible.

During the mid-'80s, while Type C was the standard format for production of studio masters and high-end editing, another format for broadcast ENG began to take root. Called 3/4-inch U-matic, it offered improved portability but with lower overall video quality. For duplicating tapes, 3/4-inch U-matic is not preferable beyond three generations.

When such small formats as 3/4-inch are used, time-base errors, instabilities in the video signal, can occur. To correct this problem, a device called the digital time-base corrector (TBC) was introduced in 1973. The Emmy Award–winning device permits broadcasters to use almost any size helical format and still meet FCC broadcast specifications.

By 1981, both Sony and JVC/Panasonic had introduced new, high-quality 1/2-inch formats for broadcast: Sony's Betacam (not to be confused with Betamax, a consumer format discontinued in 1989) and Panasonic's M format. Both formats nearly matched the quality of 1-inch Type C and redefined portability by combining a field camera and videotape recording deck (porta-pak). Eventually one-piece units—quickly dubbed camcorders—evolved. The 1/2-inch format is now used for all phases of video processing and editing. Improved versions of both 1/2-inch professional formats, with a special metal tape formulation, have been developed under the names Betacam SP and M-II, respectively. The Betacam field camera (I [02:00]) employed today is a sophisticated and costly instrument that delivers component color images and up to four channels of audio. In general, smaller-format cameras are more compact and lightweight.

The 3/4-inch format, a wonderful innovation fifteen years ago, is rarely used today for anything except playback of archival footage. Many stations are considering even smaller, more compact formats for news acquisition, such as Hi-8 or SVHS. Although use of such formats would compromise video quality, it would result in vast budget savings: an SVHS or Hi-8 three-chip camcorder cost about $10,000 in 1993, whereas a comparably outfitted Betacam system cost $45,000. Station owners feel that audiences would not view the degraded image quality as substandard or unacceptable because they have become accustomed to seeing home-video-quality footage on television. In addition, many television news pundits have long believed that the appeal of television news is primarily content driven, and the technological aesthetic is something few audiences ever consider. Hi-8 or SVHS could be used in the studio as source material for editing to Betacam, or it could be "bumped up" to Betacam.

New format technologies will soon be available—such as high-definition television (HDTV), digital tape, and disc information storage—but the cost of retooling a station's equipment to employ the latest innovations represents a large investment that few local news operations can afford. Some owners feel that the costs will have to drop significantly before they can make any commitment to these new technologies.

HDTV is not yet widely available, partly because a standardized transmission format has not been adopted by the FCC. Several companies are competing for the industry-standard delivery system, and more time is needed for this new broadcast format to stabilize. Digital HDTV equipment—cameras and decks—while impressive in terms of specs and performance, tend to be very power-hungry, and therefore are not yet suited for widespread field use. Planned reductions in power consumption will allow the integration of the new digital equipment (without making all of a station's old equipment obsolete).

An intermediate step is a machine that will play both original Betacam and the new digital Betacam formats. Currently, video engineers have a wait-and-see attitude toward a complete digital retooling. Plans are to continue to use Betacam for acquisition, cuts-only editing, and postproduction (editing with transitions that include dissolves and wipes, graphics, overlays, Ampex Digital Optics [ADO], and other special effects).

Harry Fuller of KPIX in San Francisco feels that this conversion will *not* be resisted. "It will be phased in just as video-tape was to replace film. This time it will be driven as much by a desire to eliminate jobs and costs as by anything else" (personal correspondence).

AUDIO

A popular and efficient setup of audio consoles and switchers employs a console mixing thirty-two inputs and the Grass Valley 300 switcher. Electret condenser microphones are industry standard, while Lectrosonics, Sennheiser, Vega, Sony, and Telex are all used for wireless deployments. It is imperative that any wireless mic sound as natural as a wired one. Also, radio frequency (RF) signal strength should be strong enough to span the distances between locations. Today's wireless systems are compact and extremely dependable.

LIGHTING

In general, local news broadcasting utilizes an enhanced three-point lighting setup because the news announcers do not move from their desk-set. The lighting array for a news broadcast set, in that sense, rarely changes. In the past, black-and-white cameras required "high key" lighting, which produced at least 500 foot-candles of illumination. High key lighting took lots of fill-light in relation to key and had fairly high lighting levels overall—few shadows, hard edges, and high contrast. Today news sets have a softer look, achieved by new low-lux solid-state-chip cameras. As a result, the average set can be illuminated to no more than 100–125 foot-candles. Compared to the method of lighting late '50s variety shows, such as "The Lawrence Welk Show," at more than 1,600 foot-candles (the equivalent of solar radiation at high noon), it is not surprising that performers appeared flat—in more ways than one.

The average modern studio employs a lighting control system with forty-five to sixty separate circuits. A control console, called a dimmer board, is programmed to store setups on a computer, maintaining consistent and predictable lighting. In addition, the computer can record and store an entire set of lighting presets, which can be coded and recalled almost instantly, depending on the requirements of the set. One anchorperson, for example, may require a different lighting array than another. Soft lighting units, called soft boxes, are 2,000-

watt fixtures with a flat white reflector: the reflected light, rather than direct light from the lamp, illuminates the set. Other lights deployed are called Fresnels, named for the special plano-convex lens that helps them achieve sharp focus. Both of these fixtures employ tungsten bulbs and come in 2,000- and 5,000-watt sizes. Other units include familiar scoops and ellipsoidal spotlights, commonly manufactured by Mole-Richardson, Strand Century, DeSisti, and others.

The set lighting for a news broadcast should be free of glare or backlight wash, which may disrupt the use of the TelePrompTers. Lighting flares in the device's mirrors make words unreadable, so the talent cannot read their script.

The newest lighting technology replaces the standard incandescent bulbs with gas-discharge bulbs similar to fluorescent lamps. The new, spectrally balanced bulbs operate at several kilohertz (normal lamps operate at 60 hertz), which eliminates lamp flickering on videotape and provides the correct color balance for CCD chip studio cameras. This results in perfectly balanced color imagery with one-sixteenth the traditional heat load, which has kept newsroom sets on the warm side. Such new lamp systems also provide long-range energy savings.

ROBOTICS AND AUTOMATION

A typical nonrobotic news set employs three mobile studio cameras and three camera operators, who earn a significant salary. Robotic systems, such as the Vinten MC-100 (III [09:03]), allow one operator to program and manipulate all cameras simultaneously by use of a tablet system that employs an overlay showing symbols representing an array of camera shots. This results in a more cost-effective operation as the cost of the robot system is amortized over the time that three camera operator salaries would have been paid. This kind of automation results in a more economically sound operation, making local news more cost-efficient.

Automation has also affected the way news scripts are fed to the TelePrompTer (IV [03:47]). Scripts stored in the newsroom computer are now fed into the prompter; a human operator listens to the talent and manually scrolls the projection of the script to keep pace with the talent's delivery. Proponents of automation are looking for a way to automate this process, removing the need for a prompter operator. The most promising idea involves a voice-recognition/voice-activation module for the newsroom computer that automatically keeps the scripts rolling in sync with the talent. Another method would allow on-air talent to control their own prompters, although many news directors feel this kind of operational responsibility would prove to be a distraction.

Another manually operated device is the Chyron; the operator sits at a keyboard and types in all the type overlays or "keys" that are seen on-screen as titles, logos, and other typographic identifiers. The Chyron is the industry-standard character generator (CG), a dedicated word processor for video. It is named after the most well-known brand-name manufacturer (like Xerox for photocopies), although many other companies—such as VidiFont, 3M, and Aston—make devices comparable to the original Chyron machine (II [02:24]). Depending upon the software used, various fonts (or typefaces) can be loaded onto the television screen. The fonts are measured by height by the number of lines they occupy on the 525-line display of a TV monitor. The smallest fonts are never less than twenty lines high, and may go as high as forty-five lines for short words or phrases. The character generator also scrolls titles past the screen; the speed of the roll or crawl must be coordinated and programmed well in advance.

Automation now ties this function into the main newsroom computer by allowing reporters and story/script writers to code their text in such a way that the computer can download information and fonts directly into the Chyron. Essentially one computer communicates directly with another to get the job done. Automation and new technologies will likely continue to eliminate jobs in television, by definition a technology-driven and -dependent industry.

INTERCOM SYSTEMS

The intercommunication system is critical to the functioning of the newscast operation. Most studios use three types of intercom systems: the studio address (SA), private or phone line (PL), and interruptible foldback or feedback (IFB) systems.

The SA system allows the newscast director to communicate with anyone in the studio not on the PL, or to the crew when they are on a break. The PL allows communication between all crew members who need to speak to one another. It consists of a headset with earphones and a small microphone for talkback. The IFB system allows the newscast director or producer to speak directly with talent and communicate cues or instructions. Talent normally have small ear-implant headsets, which are so small and efficient that the average viewer does not even notice them.

THE NEWSROOM COMPUTER

A major piece of technology in any station's news operation is its newsroom computer, the electronic brain center of any newsroom (II [02:11] and [07:28]). Every task involved in gathering and delivering the news is represented on this computer in some way. The computer integrates the functions of wire-service input, archive information, electronic mail, random fax, a master Rolodex, and word processor. The entire system is networked to terminals throughout the newsroom so that everyone has access to all information. Stories being written and data from outside sources can therefore be shared by everybody.

Many producers have computers and modems at home so they can plug into the newsroom before heading to the station. This major innovation makes the "rip-and-read" racket of the wire service teletypes and manual typewriters seem like quaint images from a far-distant era.

A popular model is called the BASYS Newsroom System, which uses software running on a Digital Equipment Corporation VAX minicomputer system. BASYS offers PC-based software called Newsdesk, allowing existing PCs to be connected to the larger network without expensive hardware upgrading.

A comprehensive catalog of tasks performed with many newsroom computers includes (1) creating assignments for reporters and ENG crews; (2) scheduling the use of ENG vehicles and equipment; (3) selectively acquiring news and data from incoming wire services, CNN, and major network feeds, news about VNR feeds, other satellite hookups, and formats of network news programs and then storing it under key words; (4) word processing stories and lead-ins, plus editing and revising previous stories; (5) archiving data for later usage or reference; (6) formatting and displaying

---

Newsroom Computer Systems

Basys, Inc.
Columbine Systems, Inc.
Comprompter, Inc.
Computer Engineering Associates
Computer Prompting, Inc.
Data Center Management, Inc.
Dynatech NewStar
ICA Systems
Media Computing, Inc.

---

prompter scripts; and (7) organizing the "stack," the sequence and duration of all the stories to be broadcast.

The needs of each station's news operation are unique, so it would be surprising to find any off-the-shelf software or plug-and-run hardware that would be adaptable to every station's needs. Rather, the trend in newsroom computing has been to integrate custom software with existing hardware to create hybrid systems that fulfill the needs of each station. Many high-end facilities in major markets, like WJZ-TV in Baltimore, will soon employ advanced newsroom computers capable of such functions as storing still photos, archiving, automated character generation, closed captioning, and controlling robotic studio cams and cart machines. Stations in smaller markets may not require hardware for so many ancillary functions.

The trend toward a totally computerized newsroom began in the late '70s when CNN desired to create a reputation for managing news data in a very short amount of time. Other networks and, finally, operations on the local level followed the lead. Efficiency is the watchword in utilizing a newsroom computer system. Reporters with modems built into their notebook computers can write stories in the field and phone them into the nerve center of their station's news operation. All segments of the broadcast can be assembled, stacked, and readied for air almost automatically. The horizon grows even wider as second-generation newsroom computers look to integrate even more of a station's needs and functions—resource management, traffic, master control, and library management can all be brought under the newsroom computer network. The designers of future generations of newsroom cybernetics envision video-editing workstations being integrated into news computer terminals, so that editing will be done by and with the computer.

Library management systems are seen as a replacement for the industry-standard Betacart system, which limits traffic to forty commercials or PSAs on-line at any one time. A library system that benefits from a network with a central computer operation will have access to several hundred spots at one time. Odetics Inc., which developed specialized instrumentation for NASA before entering the broadcast technology marketplace, is a reliable and popular vendor of library systems. The Odetics system is a large random-access tape and handling storage device that acts like a video hard drive. It is a multiformat machine: it can be configured in Beta, D-3 (a 1/2-inch digital format), SVHS, Hi-8, or any cartridge format.

The downside to having a news operation so totally automated is the potential for a catastrophic power loss. Stations such as KPIX-TV in earthquake-prone San Francisco have capacity for twenty-four hours of stand-alone power generation. Security is also a major consideration for stations with totally automated studio operations. Competitors or, worse, enemies of a particular station must not be allowed even the possibility of access to a newsroom computer's vast stores of data.

Additional technology is needed for the weather segment of the local news broadcast. Weather data are divided into two systems: acquisition and presentation. A popular high-end data system from Kavouras, Inc., is employed by many stations to display cloud movement, weather maps, and so on (III [09:37]). Presentation systems, which can be very sophisticated, can be supplied by major players like Kavouras or manufactured in-house on a graphics-intensive PC system.

GRAPHICS TECHNOLOGY

Production technology employs yet another group of instruments and devices. Monitors, which are actually sophisticated television receivers, are needed in the control room to monitor every phase of the broadcast—resolution, color bal-

---

Newsroom Weather Systems

Accu-Weather
Alden Electronics
Arvin/Diamond
ESD Weather Systems
Kavouras, Inc.
WSI, Inc.

---

ance and color correction, frame composition, and signal quality—in conjunction with vectorscopes for colorimetry and waveform monitors for luminance (black-and-white) information. The average cost of a high-resolution monitor is approximately $10,000. Switchers/special effects generators and graphics workstations are responsible for giving local news broadcasts their look. A switcher (IV [09:28]) is an electronic mixing bowl that accesses and combines video from a variety of sources and uses it to create new effects. The typical switcher gets its video from diverse sources—studio cameras, archive footage, satellite feeds, still-store, character generators, graphics workstations such as Paint Box, and field videotape. Once processed, the images are stored on videotape or directly transmitted for broadcast. The visuals produced by the switcher were discussed in detail in Chapter 3.

The miracles performed at a graphics workstation are a major source of visual information for any broadcast. One of the most versatile and powerful tools at the typical workstation is the digital Paint Box. This is a computer device that manipulates video images—for example, highway signs can be removed from a scene, colors may be swapped or muted, facial characteristics altered, and so on. Paint Box, the industry-standard machine manufactured by Quantel, appeared in the early '80s. Since then, the technology has improved with the appearance of several competitive systems such as Aurora (II [03:10]), Digital F/X, and Symbolics. The system software tries to emulate traditional painting by allowing the operator (usually a trained artist) to use a stylus as a fair substitute for a pen or brush. The stylus (II (03:52]) is moved about the surface of an electro-sensitive tablet, and various electronic brushstrokes can be selected to create such effects as watercolor, oil, crayon, airbrush, and even chalk. When a Paint Box is combined with a video image processor, called "Harry," the operator can perform editing legerdemain. "Harry" can store up to seventy-five seconds of video images (2,250 frames) and change them dramatically. Nonlinear edits, slow and stop motion, as well as more traditional cutting and pasting can all be viewed in real time. The images in all cases are two-dimensional, that is, they are flat just like a drawing on paper. Some systems, such as Wavefront, Vertigo, and Alias, transcend the 3D capabilities of the Paint Box.

Video animation is another workstation function that provides interesting visual information. Silicon Graphics workstations provide the power and flexibility to create high-level animation. Animation on videotape is a new process and very different from animation on film. Traditional film animation requires twenty-four individual paintings or drawings for each second of real-time motion (one Disney animated film employed more than 130,000 separate drawings). A computer-assisted animation program can simplify the process by filling in movement and information between each major change in the animated sequence. A popular system by Aurora can create animation and prepare it for immediate review, revision, and fine-tuning. This is not possible with traditional animation techniques.

Still-frame storage units are also useful components of a workstation (IV [22:11]). Known as still-store, this digital machine stores individual frames of video images on a digital hard disk or tape. By coding the frames into a database, any single frame can be recalled instantly and inserted into a story being edited to tape or broadcast directly. This system revolutionized mass storage and virtually eliminated the need for a film slide library or art cards.

The modern graphics workstation has changed how producers think about processing visual information. One of the most dramatic differences is videotape's total replacement of film. In past decades, no television station could operate without a Telecine facility—which converted film (either motion pictures or slides) to video. Today, most stations are thinking of scrapping their Telecine equipment altogether; there is simply no longer any use for film in the television news business.

When motion picture film is needed, most news operations find it more cost-effective to farm out the work to a postproduction facility with a Rank Flying Spot Scanner.

POSTPRODUCTION

Postproduction (usually called post) is what happens to videotape after all acquisition and cutting have been done. Any additional changes, such as graphics, insertions, Chyrons, animation, keys, are made in the station's post room (III [11:55]). After a station gets its network news feed (containing the national and international news), it is sent to the post room where it can be edited, packaged, and dressed for the station's nonlocal segment (or "World Wrap"). In addition, any special reports that a station may produce, such as an ongoing investigation or a multipart feature, will be assembled and enhanced in the post room using many of the machines and devices discussed throughout this chapter. With the innovations of the last decade, the postproduction process has been able to adopt many film-style production techniques. Many producers have long believed that a true "film look" is superior. Though most of what is shot for ENG employs a single camera, many field camera operators have learned enough about film-style production to capture the variety of shots needed to assemble stories. Material necessary for continuity ("seamless" editing)—master shots, cover shots, and reestablishing shots—provide videotape editors with the footage necessary to create a film-style production. This technique was employed in the videotape that accompanies this book; its benefits to the narrative are readily apparent.

NONLINEAR EDITING

Today postproduction is being revolutionized by desktop video—random-access nonlinear editing equipment and software specifically designed for the television newsroom, such as Avid's NewsCutter and similar systems from Imix and Silicon Graphics. These dedicated systems will forever change the way video news editors conceive of their work in much the same way that word processing changed the way writers conceive of theirs. In fact desktop video will replace most videotape in the newsroom, just as videotape replaced motion picture film in the 70s. All information will be stored in a compressed digital format.

To fully appreciate why nonlinear editing is so revolutionary, one must first understand traditional linear videotape editing. To edit video, material must be copied in a specific order from a first-generation cassette to a second-generation cassette. Each drop point, or edited sequence, once selected and committed to the master tape, cannot be altered without recutting the entire program.

Random-access capability for all video images or frames allows the editor to change instantly any part of a story. The process is nonlinear: the editor no longer wastes time waiting for a tape to shuttle through unproductive footage. The complete Avid digital newsgathering system consists of three broadcast products: NewsCutter, AirPlay, and Media Recorder.

NewsCutter ensures that there is almost no generation loss during the editing process and provides full 50/60 field digital video with four channels of CD-quality, 48-kHz audio. In addition, it also offers A/B-roll–style editing now found on systems like the CMX. NewsCutter also has titling and super capabilities, previously available only with the Chyron.

AirPlay is a disk-based playback system dedicated to simplifying the process of creating and/or changing the sequence of stories in a newscast's rundown. This system allows the producer and newscast director to react to late-breaking events or stories without compromising the show's integrity.

Media Recorder is a capture-and-storage device that replaces videotape as a storage and recording medium.

Digital newsgathering systems will undoubtedly create pressure on writers to become more visually literate, to understand the function and tradition of film and video editing as they combine with narration to tell an effective story. In fact, Harry Fuller envisions the following scenario: "The writer-editor-producer will be an animal of the future, and tape editors who have no other skills will join the Linotype setters and layout editors in the dustbin" (personal correspondence).

ELECTRONIC NEWSGATHERING

Electronic newsgathering, or ENG, employs camcorders to acquire field images for editing. ENG is augmented by microwave relays, satellites, helicopters, and fiber optics. Ter-restrial microwave is the most direct, inexpensive, and easiest manner to get information from one point to another. Unfor-tunately, since microwaves travel only in a straight line, trans-mission and reception are limited to line-of-sight situations. If one thinks of a microwave transmission as the beam of a flashlight (the two are approximately the same size), the limi-tations become clear. Many stations use several trucks outfit-ted with microwave transmitters and receivers, plus receive sites and repeaters strategically deployed at key points within the broadcast region. The usual locations are on the tall build-ings in metropolitan areas or perhaps a radio station's trans-mitter tower. On a daily basis, microwave is the preferred carrier because it has proved to be cost-effective.

When a microwave signal is not feasible, stations use alternate satellite technology. Operating on both C-band (3.7 to 4.2 GHz) and KU-band (11 to 12 GHz) frequencies, sta-tions, with the aid of satellite dishes, direct their signal up through the atmosphere to a fixed-position (geosynchro-nous) satellite, where it is relayed back down to the earth to a receiver beyond line-of-sight. C-band transmissions are generally more reliable and not as sensitive to adverse weather conditions (such as heavy rain or sleet) than KU-band.

A disadvantage of C-band equipment is the need for large dishes (up to thirty feet), whereas KU-band dishes are one third the size and more transportable. KU-band trucks are more versatile because they can begin broadcasting almost as soon as they arrive at a scene. A downside to daily use of KU technology is its cost. A mobile KU-band truck costs as much as $500,000, requires highly skilled (and therefore highly paid) operators, and employs satellite time, which must also be paid for. Many stations estimate that they spend more than $1,000 just driving their KU-band truck off the lot. On the other hand, microwave transmission is basically free; four vans (I [01:33]) can be purchased for the cost of one mobile KU-band vehicle.

Harry Fuller notes: "Helicopters are a common and crucial newsgathering tool, as the Reginald Denny assault trial has proved. That video would not have been possible without a helicopter. We often use helicopters to receive and retransmit microwave signals, thereby enlarging our microwave cover-age area" (personal correspondence).

Another option for acquiring live video transmission is fiber optics, the next step up from the copper cables that carry electricity and telephone transmissions. The major difference between standard and fiber-optic cable is the way the signals are carried. Standard cables use electrical energy; fiber optics use light. Since light waves travel 186,234 miles per second, they can carry millions of data bits per second; yet the glass or plastic cable (or fiber) is no thicker than a human hair. By bundling many of these fibers together into more standard-looking, insulated, and protected cables, thousands of separate communications can be carried simultaneously.

Fiber optics appears to be more than adequate for transmitting video compression data. Video compression is a way to process the digitized information about an image and encode it in such a way that it requires less storage space. Pioneers in this technology include JPEG, DVI, and MPEG. Harry Fuller looks to the near future, when "video compression will allow sending of live signals over a cell-phone. You will see a whole new generation of technical jumps in speed and distance for local news coverage." He foresees this to be a major business event that could possibly wrest TV technological leadership away from Japan and return it to the United States. "This generation of change will be more software-driven than hardware-driven. Just as Microsoft is now more important than IBM in setting the future direction of computer use, Silicon Graphics will be more important than Sony in setting the future path of TV operations" (personal correspondence).

In addition, fiber-optic transmissions are immune to standard interference, and there is no leakage, corrosion, or short-circuiting. As telephone companies retool their industry to use fiber optics exclusively, coast-to-coast video transmission will be as easy and cost-effective as plugging video or computer equipment into a phone line and dialing a phone number. The need for unwieldy microwave or costly satellite technologies will be practically eliminated.

MASTER CONTROL

Utilizing a switcher similar in design to the routing/production switcher examined earlier, master control handles selections of all the video and audio from various sources, including commercial inserts. It can simultaneously switch audio and video (called audio-follow-video) to the transmitter and can perform its functions with split-second accuracy. Such accuracy can be crucial because revenue can be lost when commercials do not air as scheduled. With the advent of multichannel sound, most stations had to be completely retooled to accommodate stereophonic audio.

Video information must be gathered, processed, and delivered to the station's transmitter and then to the audience clearly and cleanly. The power of the transmitter depends somewhat on the size of the DMA, but many stations use such equipment as the solid-state Harris series. Today transmitters can operate at lower power levels by utilizing efficient antennas (see the opening credits on the accompanying videotape).

DIRECT BROADCAST SATELLITE

Developed by Hubbard Broadcasting, direct broadcast satellite (DBS) will begin broadcasting cable TV–type programming from a satellite owned by GM Hughes Electronics to inexpensive eighteen-inch home satellite dishes and signal decoders. This new service will compete head-to-head for customers with the cable TV industry and will service rural areas where cable is not available. The effect of this new technology on local newsgathering is still uncertain, but it will certainly penetrate new potential markets (see Gross).

CONCLUSION

In summary, current electronic technology is playing an increasing role in the way local news is gathered, produced, and broadcast. Technology has caused station engineers and management to reevaluate the cost of doing business. Many innovations have resulted in enormous budgetary savings by the elimination of wasteful tasks and excess personnel; but others (such as HDTV and digital videotape) may prove too expensive to warrant their adoption by many local news operations. With the highly trumpeted expansion of the cable TV marketplace into as many as 500 channels, it seems unlikely that any station could ever hope to garner a large enough share of the audience to be economically successful. If the costs of new technology do not decrease quickly enough, many new techniques and machines will not be adopted. When one considers the product (local news productions), a station can quickly reach a point of diminishing returns when purchasing new technologies. More than one industry has fallen prey to the temptation to try killing flies with laser cannons when a simple fly swatter would suffice. *How good does it have to be?* The answer to that question becomes more significant with each passing year and with each new channel.

Indeed, the local television news industry is fast approaching a "techno-economic barrier," a state beyond which many stations will either excel into the next century or self-destruct in a display of overpriced and overextended pieces of machinery.

5

A Case Study:
WJZ-TV, Channel 13, Baltimore

A BRIEF HISTORY

Channel 13, Baltimore, whose original call letters were WAAM-TV, first broadcast on November 2, 1948, carrying the results of the 1948 presidential election. Owned by Ben and Herman Cohen and jointly affiliated with both the American Broadcasting Company and the Dumont Network, the station at first produced very little original programming. Early efforts included "The Johns Hopkins Science Review," "Shopping For You," "Home Cooking," "The Fourth Man," and a documentary series called "Focal Point." The majority of the locally produced material was informational, rather than entertainment oriented.

In the 1950s WAAM clearly emphasized quality public-service programming. For more than a decade, in association with the Baltimore Public School System, it produced a series of educational programs for classroom instruction throughout the city. The station also pioneered the local broadcasting of live sporting events by carrying the Baltimore Colts football games from 1954 to 1956.

The earliest daily newscast at WAAM was presented at 7:20 p.m. and ran for only ten minutes. There was no real set—just a tight shot from a single camera of an announcer with a clock behind his shoulder. There was no TelePrompTer: the announcer sat on a stool and held his script, typewritten in double-spaced caps. It was difficult to read, but there was no alternative at the time.

The news department comprised three people: the announcer, a film-shooter/producer, and a freelance shooter (cameraman). The cameramen used one news car, each day driving all over the city of more than a million people, believing that they were covering every significant event in the region.

WAAM's affiliation with Dumont ceased in 1956, and ABC became the sponsoring network. Soon after, the station was sold to the Westinghouse Broadcasting Company (Group W), in June 1957. After the ownership changed, the call letters and logo also changed: WAAM-TV became WJZ-TV. The new management increased the station's commitment to broadcast more news programming, including the now-familiar triad of news, weather, and sports.

Group W hired the best newscaster in the area, Keith McBee, who appeared on an improved set (but still spartan by today's standards) that featured a world map in the background. George Bauman also began as a local news commentator at this time. The news staff was enlarged almost immediately, and the newscast was expanded to a half hour. The station became the first Baltimore channel to employ a full-time editorial director.

Videotape was just emerging in the early 1960s; film was still the major source of visual material. But film lacked sound, so when announcers cued the film, studio engineers always added "dramatic" music to the footage. The audio technician would pull a disk from the station's sound-effects library as the director would ask for a particular type of music—happy, serious, religious. Scenes of fatal auto accidents, for example, were always accompanied by funereal strains.

Local news was also used as rip-and-read filler during breaks between dance sequences on the popular afternoon rock-'n'-roll disk jockey programs—local variations on Dick Clark's "American Bandstand." Political coverage at this time was minimal; the major topics were fires, accidents, homicides—and there were only six reporters to cover everything. George Bauman recalls arranging for a conductor on the Pennsylvania Railroad to carry film footage from New York down to Baltimore each afternoon. Sometimes there was no time to edit the film and material was just thrown onto a reel and inserted into the broadcast.

When Joe Templeton became the anchor, the set was further improved with the addition of a camera and a rear-projection screen, showing slides of downtown Baltimore as background. In the early '60s, Allen Smith became the anchor at 11:00 p.m., while the 6:00 p.m. show was anchored by Jerry Turner. In one of the earliest confirmations of the validity of ratings in local news, the phenomenal appeal of Turner became evident when the 6:00 p.m. news rated higher than the late-night show. When Turner was switched to the 11:00 p.m. slot, ratings soared for the late news and plummeted for the 6:00 p.m. newscast. With the dominance of Jerry Turner as the anchor of the "Eyewitness News" program in 1964, WJZ acquired its first and most well-respected "personality." The following year Wiley Daniels became the first African-American reporter to join the staff.

The mid- to late '60s saw the evolution of newscasting into what was pejoratively called happy talk news—all the on-air personalities would smile and have pleasant (but often banal) conversations instead of delivering hard news. The format received almost universally bad reviews from television critics and analysts, but during this time the news staff tripled within a few years and the emphasis on quality news programming increased.

WJZ-TV continued to produce original programming, especially public-affairs shows. Over the years it was awarded some of the industry's most prestigious honors: the Ohio State Award, the Gabriel, and the Columbia DuPont. In 1976 the station further emphasized its commitment to news by expanding the 6:00 p.m. show to one hour. An investigative team and consumer reporter were also added to the burgeoning staff. In 1977 "Evening Magazine," a ground-breaking soft news show, debuted on WJZ-TV.

The trend toward more local news and public-affairs programming continued at WJZ into the 1980s. Reflecting the changes at other large-DMA stations around the country, and recognizing the success of formats such as "Evening Magazine," WJZ began emphasizing more features and specials in its daily programming and less hard news. Since today the station continues to enjoy the highest ratings in the Baltimore market, management sees no reason to change its successful philosophy or format.

This case study attempts to draw a profile of WJZ-TV that is larger than the sum of its parts. Each aspect of the local news operation is examined in detail, creating a mosaic of the station and providing the reader a comprehensive understanding of how local news is gathered, edited, produced, and ultimately broadcast.

GENERAL MANAGER

The power to make all major decisions regarding local news operations resides with the highest management levels of WJZ-TV. The station employs experienced, professional department heads, but one individual, the general manager, is charged with seeing the big picture. Marcellus Alexander, WJZ's vice president and general manager, must identify his station's short- and long-range priorities. He is not, however, expected to be an expert in every aspect of broadcasting, but he must have a *general* working knowledge of all departments. Like an orchestra conductor, he need not know how to play every instrument, but he must know what each instrument can do.

Alexander began working in electronic media as an account executive for WRIF-FM radio in Detroit. He was eventually promoted to general sales manager and then vice president and general manager. He ended up becoming one of the station's owners when the FCC required its previous owners to divest from some of its communications holdings. Eventually Alexander moved to television and became station manager at KYW-TV in Philadelphia, where he worked until he was promoted to his present position at WJZ.

The GM is paid to make the tough decisions, to solve the impossible problems, and to face whatever crisis might arise with his staff. He must ensure that all his department chiefs work well together with a minimum of personality friction. He must also answer to the station's stockholders and owners when profits are reported. The difference between great management and good management determines whether a station is one of the most successful, with profit margins of 35 to 40 percent, or one of the many that earn 25 to 34 percent. The industry in general is not as lucrative now as in the early years of television broadcasting.

In most businesses, the buck stops there, but broadcasting is special. Alexander must answer not only to his corporate bosses, but also to the FCC, the federal agency that issues WJZ's license. Thus, the GM shoulders responsibility for making money while also serving the public interest, convenience, and necessity.

By the nature of the position, the GM has no typical or routine day. The department chiefs handle all the expected problems and duties; the GM helps work through the *unex*pected ones. This includes interacting with community organizations, corporate interests, and WJZ's advertisers. There is a lot of mail to answer and lots of phone calls to return. He must be aware of the dynamic aspect of broadcasting—nothing ever remains the same—and that broadcasting takes its energy from things always changing. Alexander must stay abreast of changes inside WJZ as well as outside the station: in the community at large, at competing stations in the Baltimore DMA, and to a lesser extent, at stations around the country.

Alexander believes that WJZ is not being influenced or compromised by recent trends toward the tabloid format or the quick-cut, music-video style of such stations as WSVN in Miami. Each market has its own personality, its own set of responses to a particular presentation, and there is no reason to believe that the hot, jazzy, extremely sensationalized style of WSVN is at all compatible with the Baltimore marketplace.

Although WJZ-TV is part of Group W, a wholly owned subsidiary of Westinghouse Broadcasting Company, Inc., the parent corporation is not necessarily involved in the day-to-day operations of the station. Group W has five stations under its umbrella (WBZ, Boston; KDKA, Pittsburgh; KPIX, San Francisco; KYW, Philadelphia; and WJZ, Baltimore), and each functions independently. To ensure the variety and vitality that comes from maintaining individuality, Group W avoids the cookie-cutter mentality that would insist upon all five of its stations looking and acting in undifferentiated ways. Marcellus Alexander therefore has a free hand to give WJZ its own personality, look, and direction.

Alexander must also be concerned with the station's relationship with each of the many unions that represent the skilled personnel at the station. In recent years, with economic pressures resulting in streamlined techniques and downsized staffs, the unions have become more understanding of management's challenge to not only remain competitive, but also to be profitable.

In terms of ratings and market shares, WJZ-TV's 6:00 a.m. morning news generates a 40-plus share and is therefore an excellent lead-in for ABC's "Good Morning America." The station's overall ranking for all its news programming is a strong number one. In the evening, WJZ's "Eyewitness News" and ABC's "World News Tonight" have complemented each other very well. Alexander is well aware that the "Eyewitness News" organization has one of WJZ's largest budgets. More than any other programming, news shows project the station's significant leadership image in the public eye.

In fact, the open lines of communication with Baltimore-area leaders provide Alexander with a major source of feedback. The FCC's guidelines have termed this sort of policy Community Ascertainment. Holding regularly scheduled meetings with community representatives is an important part of the GM's duties. He needs to know their opinions about which problems facing the community are the most important; the content and direction of WJZ's local news programming; and how to improve not only the station's services to the community, but also its working relationship with citizens. Alexander feels a responsibility to remain in touch with not just the region's officials, but also the people in the streets, the average members of the audience. As one of the few African-American general managers in the country, he is especially mindful of the needs of WJZ's minority audiences.

To ensure the best possible news operation, Marcellus Alexander, like most station GMs, hires "news doctors" or consultants. Such independent market-research firms help analyze WJZ's news programs and suggest policies and strategies that may attract a wider audience. Consultants such as Frank N. Magid and Associates, one of the largest news doctors in the country, figure into the overall plan of WJZ's operations.

It is believed that any local news unit can benefit from the less-subjective points of view and fresher suggestions of a consultant than those of the inner circle of the regular production staff. Consultants discuss programming in terms of content, presentation, promotion, set design, and the chemistry, appeal, and delivery of on-air personalities. In fact, some consultants act as talent agencies by recommending individuals from other markets.

As new technology continues to increase viewers' options, a station must identify its strengths to grow in a highly competitive marketplace. Alexander believes that WJZ's niche is in broadcasting local news and information with excellence; he has committed the station's resources to building upon that reputation.

NEWS DIRECTOR

The person at WJZ who decides what will get on the air each day is news director Gail Bending. She manages a staff of forty-seven people—including anchors, writers, producers, camera operators, and reporters. She assigns, personally or through subordinates, the tasks necessary to gather the news and air it. She works directly with her assistant, the operations manager, to see that all the staff members have weekly schedules and assignments.

Each day she must review and analyze her news sources—field reporters out in the community, local agencies and government offices sending in advance notices of events and policies, anonymous tips and calls from community members, and piles of periodicals, newspapers, press releases, and more. She also has an investigative unit of journalists, who are always probing beneath the surface of events for hidden stories. Bending and her assignment editor and producers decide the newsworthiness of material and who on the staff will cover each story. All input from photographers and reporters is welcome, but the news director is ultimately responsible for the maintenance of WJZ-TV's total news philosophy. When people think of Channel 13's "Eyewitness News," it is Gail Bending's conceptualization that comes to mind.

In general, the newsroom encounters more material than it can cover in any single broadcast. Therefore, decisions must be made as to what will be kept and what will be passed over.

These decisions are usually roundtabled with Bending's news management team and other members of her support staff. Availability of tape footage, number of field reporters, and relevance to the community are all factors contributing to the final decisions.

Bending must also consider the competition—the other stations in the Baltimore DMA. She has three television monitors in her office tuned to the other major stations, and she must watch them carefully to keep abreast of what stories they are covering. She must always ask herself: Have we missed anything important? How is our coverage different and better than what the other stations are doing?

In terms of staff management, Bending monitors Channel 13's newscasts to ensure that they are always consistent with the "Eyewitness News" philosophy. She always listens carefully to the copy for the anchors to ensure that there are no mispronunciations and is ever watchful for too much editorializing from a reporter preparing a story. She is constantly assessing the work of her entire department to make sure it is being done properly and to look for ways to improve.

Bending learned her job by gathering experience from a host of other positions in television. Starting as an intern in college, she moved on to a full-time position as an assignment editor, then as a producer. Eventually she became the department's executive producer, and assumed the duties of the news director several years ago. Having remained in one city for the duration of her career is rare. Many high-level television department chiefs have traveled not only up the positional ladder but also from station to station, usually moving from a smaller market to a larger one.

Ten years ago the majority of news directors were white men in their thirties. Since that time the industry has seen an influx of women taking on the duties of news directors, and Bending believes the trend will continue because many of the television staffers who become producers tend to be female. Frequently, television news directors gain important experience as producers and then move on to join the station's middle-management team.

A typical day for Gail Bending begins around 7:30 a.m. when she watches "Good Morning America" to see if anything has changed on the national or international fronts that might supersede local interests. She prepares herself for the "morning calls," conference calls with her staff. The calls serve as a kind of preplanning session, when everyone gets a chance to suggest story ideas and events that merit coverage. She relies on her executive producer and producer to flesh out the format they loosely construct each morning on these calls. Unless things become controversial as the planning of the day progresses, Bending assumes her delegated tasks are being carried out as planned.

After arriving at the studio, she chairs a morning meeting in which everyone attempts to refine the topics and elements introduced during the conference call. They also deal with the regularly scheduled features, such as health, consumer troubleshooting, and education segments. The most important decision to make at this time is what will be the lead story. Also, what topic merits the team coverage, and what will be the kicker? Bending believes that it is important to know as early as possible how the show will end.

As the day evolves, her main task is to determine the optimum mix for that day's broadcast. She attempts to step back and look at the material as objectively as possible to determine what the show's feel might be that day. An experienced news director learns to take the pulse of her own show. She is always concerned with making the content interesting and lively. If her story material is important or vital but the story is basically dry because it lacks what she calls "real people," she may need to cover it using a different angle or slant.

After the morning meeting, she delegates responsibilities to her staff and turns to concerns that have more long-range impact on news production at WJZ. She usually meets with other department chiefs, in creative services, engineering, sales, and of course with general manager Alexander. By late afternoon she tries to attend the production meeting, where she may be asked to proof a controversial story. The more routine proofings are handled by her executive producer and assistant news director.

Usually there are stories breaking during the course of the day that cannot be planned at any of the daytime meetings; as the 6:00 p.m. show prepares to air, staff members are also working on the late-breaking material for the 11:00 p.m. broadcast. By the time she is ready to quit for the day, Bending usually has time to at least touch base with the late-night news staff. Unless there is a very hot, late-breaking event, Bending relies on her support staff to deal with the 11:00 p.m. broadcast.

Bending believes that her staff is a good one, that everyone knows his or her job and what is expected. She does not want to have everyone else standing around waiting for her to approve every task and decision. She prides herself in having a news staff that has been given the confidence to take charge when necessary.

The future of her position as news director carries extra responsibility. There is growing need to take an active part in the fiscal stability of the station. In the past, when problems were perceived in any station's operations, not just WJZ's, the immediate solution was to throw some additional people and money at it. In today's economy, even a news director must think more like a business manager. Financial restraints have become a part of every station's day-to-day life, and Bending must focus some of her energy on how her decisions will affect the station's budget. One of the major ways to save money is to reduce the size of a news operation's staff; that translates into getting fewer people to do more work. In the controlled chaos of a studio newsroom, this strategy may not always be the wisest.

Another consideration for the future is maintaining viewer loyalty; with each passing month it seems as though the viewer enjoys more and more choices of not only entertainment but also information. In past decades there were perhaps two other newscasts and two other sets of anchors with which to compete. But with the onset of cable programming and the mean and lean local cable news operations, plus the advent of fiber optics and interactive television, viewers will be able to program their television activities hours or days in advance.

An interesting graphic innovation that reflects the changing times for television news is the small logo "bug" that appears in the corner of the screen almost constantly during a newscast. CNN is credited with employing the logo first, but other stations—WJZ included—soon learned its benefit. Viewers armed with remote controls that allow them to flip through channels in an instant can nevertheless see the little logo bug on the screen. It helps keeps people watching if they know instantly what they are indeed watching.

Gail Bending realizes that her news operation will have to be better than it was in the past because the competition, if not better, is at least more plentiful. The onus of responsibility for viewer loyalty and retention does not reside solely with the news director, but Bending is keenly aware of her role in not only the content of her newscasts but also their appeal to the audience.

EXECUTIVE PRODUCER

Being the executive producer means working long hours. It means being responsible for the daily newscast from its conception to its slow birth at the wrap of the 11:00 p.m. broadcast. Helene King (III [04:36]) is the executive producer of the night edition of WJZ-TV's local news. She works closely with almost everyone associated with the show's production: the producer, reporters, assignment editors, anchors, and newscast director. Her day is punctuated by meetings with these staff members, but her duties encompass much more.

When a story requires that a particular element be covered, King decides what type of treatment a story will get. She also decides what story will need a reporter to accompany the camera operator or what will be video-only.

The executive producer's day begins at home by 9:30 a.m. First she reviews the "futures file," a list of stories preplanned for the coming day's broadcasts. She also spends time reading through the morning newspapers—she is always looking for new story ideas and new angles on prospective stories. Next she watches the noon newscasts of the competing stations to ensure that her station has not missed or overlooked anything important. She again reviews the futures, sometimes adding to or subtracting from the list.

King must also attend a variety of administrative meetings within her own department as well as with other department heads on a weekly basis. This is required of all employees who are part of a station's management team. There may also be personnel matters that fall under King's purview.

By 3:00 p.m., she confers with her reporters and producer; it is the first full meeting in preparation for the 11:00 p.m. newscast. She has only two reporters available for the late broadcast, so the stories they cover must be carefully chosen.

It is important to decide how much time each story is given. A lead in the A Section (the first of five sections in the 11:00 p.m. newscast) can get from 1:30 to 2:00 minutes. King realizes from feedback and viewer input that the 11:00 p.m. audience is most interested in catching up on local happenings, but national and international stories are also important.

Then she sits in on the final meeting for the 6:00 p.m. broadcast, always looking for items or stories that might merit a follow-up or spinoff during the 11:00 p.m. edition. It is unusual for her to plan a follow-up story with a completely new package and a new reporter. Nonlocal stories must also be examined to see if there are any connections to the city or the state, such as victims in train wrecks or plane crashes. King is always looking for the story that typifies the goals of "Eyewitness News," the emotional look that touches viewers and is important to them.

King also joins her producer, Margaret Cronan, in reading through the wire-service material for any other news possibilities. They subscribe to the idea that there will be less chance of overlooking a story if two people are responsible rather than one. King also packages a daily segment called "Maryland Day in Review," a quick wrap of secondary stories done as fifteen-second pieces from the 6:00 p.m. newscast and stories that were cut for various reasons. Once she writes this package, it is taken to the post room for editing and assembly.

The executive producer is also responsible for the teasers that air during prime time. She writes and assembles a thirty-second spot that will highlight the late edition's most interesting stories. With the possibility of late-breaking events changing the content of the newscast, King must stay as close to the pulse of the city as possible. She must remain in touch with her producer and her reporters almost constantly. As the evening wears on, she spends time with her producer, reviews reporters' scripts and stories written by the associate producer. This is the crucial time when everything scheduled to be broadcast must be reviewed one last time for accuracy and a conversational writing style.

For any given newscast, King deals with twenty-two minutes of broadcast time. The rest will be taken by sports and weather segments. King decides how the news time will be used most efficiently.

PRODUCER

Margaret Cronan (II [02:05]) is WJZ's producer on the 11:00 p.m. news broadcast. Because the duties of her position are so highly structured, it will be informative and enlightening to examine a typical day in her life.

Cronan's day at the station begins around 3:00 p.m. and does not wrap up until midnight. Her first obligation is to catch up on the day's events. To do this, she meets with the assignment editor and executive producer to analyze all the material in the futures file—by now really a compilation of all significant events going on that day, in addition to the preplanned material from the previous evening. At this primary meeting, Cronan and her two colleagues decide which stories will be covered and which will be tossed out.

Once the stories have been selected, the production trio must decide how each story will be covered—for example, should the piece be a simple voiceover or should it be a full-blown package with field reporter, footage, and anchor lead-in. If full coverage is selected, then the reporters (two or three for each evening broadcast) must be assigned. Cronan attempts to adhere to a schedule that will allow each reporter to have his or her assignment package by 3:30 p.m. If the reporter is not out on the street by 4:00 p.m., then he or she should at least be making the preliminary calls—trying to find or set up a story.

Such a perfect scenario rarely occurs. Sometimes when the production team meets, there is one great story and lots of small, uninteresting events—or worse, a day with absolutely nothing happening. Cronan then has to scrape and pull and dig until something of interest comes to the forefront. She must get her reporters in motion, either out looking for a story or working on available leads, however slight.

After the meeting, Cronan goes to her office, while Donna Miller, the assignment editor, attends to routine desk duties and executive producer Helene King begins working on her preproduction checklist. Cronan monitors the wires and the ABC network feed that comes down from 4:00 to 6:00 p.m. She must be especially careful to find video for both the 6:00 p.m. and 11:00 p.m. broadcasts. More national video is needed for the late news edition, so she pays particular attention to the network feed for appropriate material. While watching the feed, she reads copy off the newswires, which provide stories that can be used as voiceovers. When the *Evening Sun* (Baltimore's major late-edition newspaper) comes in, she will also give it a quick scan to ensure that the team has not missed something. Also at this time, she may help a reporter make telephone calls, but that is normally a duty of the assignment editor.

Cronan is constantly looking for what she calls "sexy" video—material that is fresh and exciting. She looks for footage that will make the viewer say: "Oh my God . . . look at that!" or "Did you see that video on Channel 13?" For example, a fire with spectacular flames or home video of a crime or an accident in progress would be perfect. Even if the footage was shot in another city or state, if it's visually compelling, Cronan will air it.

As Cronan watches the feeds and reads the wires and newspapers, she assigns a reporter to tape a "Tonight at 11," a tease that airs during the 6:00 p.m. newscast, promoting a story that will not be covered until 11:00. This tease features a field reporter, usually at the scene of the story, revealing just enough of the story to convince people to tune in for the late broadcast.

At 6:00 p.m. Cronan takes a seat in the producer's chair, where she can monitor the first twenty minutes of the 6:00 p.m. news broadcast and check for the quality of the video being used. If she is going to use any stories from the evening show for the late-night edition, they usually come from the first ten or twenty minutes. She also monitors the 11:00 p.m. teases on the two competing network affiliates in Baltimore—a final check to make sure the other local news operations are not covering something that Channel 13 somehow missed. At 6:30 she catches the first broadcast of "World News Tonight" to check on what the network feels are the lead stories on the national and international scenes, and also to monitor the availability of any new, usable video. The network news operation usually holds video acquired late in the day for immediate broadcast; it is not included in the earlier ABC feed.

At 7:00 p.m., Cronan begins the actual formatting of the 11:00 p.m. newscast. She fills in a blank template on her computer screen (II [02:01]), choosing the lead story, what will follow, and so on. This usually takes her an hour. She then shares the format with the executive producer. Once they agree on the order, Cronan creates the "dub list," a list of all stories in the newscast that will have video accompaniment. Cronan gives each story a "slug" or title, then indicates what video must be cut: for example, if it's a voiceover, she indicates what shots to use and where the video will come from (a feed or video shot by a news team photographer). She distributes the dub list to the videotape editors so they can start cutting. The 11:00 p.m. writers and anchors also get a copy, so they will know if they need to refer to specific shots in their script.

Once the dub list is distributed, Cronan can create her late-night tease, a short promotional spot that will air just before the news begins at 11:00 p.m. She must decide which story to highlight in the tease and then alert the field reporter covering the piece that she'll need a sound bite of eight to ten seconds—revealing something interesting about the story.

By 10:15, the entire show is usually written; Cronan and her executive producer review the scripts in the computer, checking for factual and grammatical errors. After making any necessary changes, they print the script.

The half hour before showtime is critical in case a late-breaking story is still developing. If so, Cronan will be extremely pressured to reformat the broadcast. She must also apprise the director and the editors of any last-minute changes to the rundown. Everyone must be kept aware of the structure of the "stack"—the sequence and content of the stories. For example, the night the accompanying video was taped, some reformatting was required because of the late-breaking reactions to the not-guilty verdicts in the trial of the arresting officers of Rodney King. In addition, Cronan and her production team were relying on live (as it was happening) feeds from ABC affiliates and network coverage in Los Angeles. They were editing on-the-fly and running with whatever footage they could get. This kind of broadcasting, while exciting and challenging, can be fraught with stress.

During the actual broadcast, the news producer's primary job is to make sure the show gets on and off the air on time. She watches the Chyrons, trying to catch any misspellings before they get on the air; the assistant director also watches—a fail-safe system of double-checking.

Cronan times the entire show to the second because she

must be off-air at exactly 11:28:15. If for example she is one minute "heavy" (too long) at the first commercial break, she must reformat on-the-fly and take some time from the weather or drop a story from the upcoming news section, or even shave a few seconds from sports. When time is at a premium and something must be excised, the temptation is always to look to the weather segment because it is not scripted (the weather talent ad-libs everything). In addition to being punctual and precise, she strives to be as fair as possible. As producer, Cronan coordinates anything she wants to change with the newscast director while the show is running. The pace is hectic, the atmosphere full of high pressure. Live shots coming in on a *very* late-breaking story are also the producer's call. With almost no time to decide, Cronan must appraise the quality of the live signal and video and either take the shot or kill it. (In the video accompanying this text, the careful listener can hear staff calling for "Net One" or "Net Two"; these are references to live feeds coming into the station directly from ABC headquarters.)

In addition to her daily duties, Cronan also looks for new sources of news for her station. It pays to be a "news junkie"— someone who loves to read, especially newspapers and periodicals. The best news producers are truly concerned about the community, and constantly ask questions about the world around them.

NEWSCAST DIRECTOR

The job of Guy Raymond (II [01:52]), the newscast director at WJZ, is combination traffic cop, technical coordinator, and program juggler. He is responsible for seeing that the hourlong 6:00 p.m. and the half-hour 11:00 p.m. newscasts take place precisely as planned. He works closely with the producer to ensure that the format and story stack are carried out without any glitches. While his job is in high-profile during the on-air sessions at 6:00 and 11:00 p.m., the newscast director must spend many more hours each day planning, organizing, and delegating tasks. A typical daily newscast is like a jigsaw puzzle. It comprises many elements that must be gathered together and pieced into something cohesive and intelligible. The newscast director is the person who assembles the puzzle.

Raymond's daily schedule is defined by a series of meetings, the first of which is the production meeting with the producer, the talent, and the writers. At this meeting the newscast director receives the day's format, which is then analyzed story by story, so that the writers will know where to go for the information on each story in the stack, and also to give the talent some initial familiarity with the material they will be reading on-air.

At this time, Raymond begins to fill in the plans and instructions that will make the format come to life (II [01:49]). He assigns videotape machines to each story. He must also determine the camera assignments—that is, what camera will be covering what talent, especially when dealing with feature and special-report appearances. Something as simple as what seat will be used (for example, the weather seat or the sports seat) is critical information that needs to be mapped out well in advance of broadcast time. The newscast director must also account for any planned live shots; he needs to know the source of the live material—whether it's microwave, satellite, or network feed—so that the proper technicians are alerted to see that the respective shots join the broadcast at a specific time.

Once he has a general picture of the form and content of the newscast, Raymond begins taking the steps necessary to ensure that it is correctly assembled from the various sources—the jigsaw puzzle takes shape. Formats must be generated for the ENG control operator—a combination flowchart and instruction sheet detailing the names and sequence of the tapes scheduled to be played, plus the source machines for each tape. Raymond will also at this time confer with both his technical director and his audio operator to confirm the format and note any special situations. He also confirms the format personally with the video operator who controls microwave live shots or satellite uplinks or downlinks.

The first step is to put together a preproduction file. Raymond decides with the producer what graphics are needed, or if any special effects, artwork, Chyrons, or over-the-shoulder boxes need to be prebuilt and readied for insertion during the broadcast. For example, violators, the lower-third banners with Chyron text keyed over a videotape (II [05:00] and IV [04:13]), may be needed.

The next task is to prepare a rundown of still-stores for the technical director—so that the TD can provide all the visuals the producer selected. Once this is done, it is time to print the script. When Raymond has a script in hand, he marks it according to the information he has written on the format. He then uses it as his blueprint and a checklist to collect all the final information for the newscast; then the still-store list, rundown, and script all go to the control room. The goal is to create a neat, cohesive package on schedule with everyone knowing what's going on far enough in advance to ensure a smooth operation. Invariably, however, there is a late-breaking story, such as a triple shooting or an eight-alarm fire, that causes all plans to be revised. A perfect example can be seen on the accompanying videotape, when live network feed kept the video operators very busy and caused much of the prewritten material to be killed.

Once the actual broadcast begins, the newscast director works side by side with the producer to see that everyone follows the format. Raymond likes to try to stay one or two steps ahead of the broadcast so that any problems or glitches can be discovered or anticipated. If he can do so, he has a good chance of circumventing or even fixing the foul-up. Format changes and technical difficulties are part of the job, and the newscast director must know how to handle them whenever they arise. If he loses a camera in the middle of the broadcast, he must deal with it.

If everything is going smoothly, Raymond can stay on top of the script, relaying cues through his mic and headset, while he stays ahead of the show. He stays in touch with the stage manager so he can revise the format if the show is running too long and something needs to be killed, or if the weather needs to be cheated down.

Raymond must do two shows per day—6:00 p.m. and 11:00 p.m. After the evening edition, he meets with the executive producer for a "postmortem" meeting, in which they review the show, with an eye toward cleaning up any writing problems or technical foul-ups. It has been customary to have at least one live shot every night, so Raymond provides for that inevitability, which usually employs a reporter on the scene.

In essence the newscast director is also like an orchestra conductor. Instead of sheet music and scores of musicians, Guy Raymond has a broadcast format and a staff of technical and on-air personnel. He coordinates the activities of everyone so that they are working in concert.

ANCHOR

The most visible positions at any news station are the ones occupied by the talent—the on-air announcers, commentators, and personalities. And of all the talent, the most highly recognizable are the people known as anchors. Their title describes what they do in the most basic way—they are the centerpiece of the entire newscast, holding everything else in place as all the stories, visuals, and even commercials cascade across the screen. On the majority of large-market stations, there are usually two anchors, sometimes three; they usually represent both sexes, and tend to be evenly distributed according to race. Anchors tend to be very well paid compared to other production team members—so well paid that critics of the industry often question why a glorified reader should be paid five to ten times more than other production staff members. The idea that such gross salary imbalances cause unrest and division among employees is also a popular one among media analysts. Many anchors themselves do not, understandably, perceive this as a problem and feel that anyone in any job will accept the highest salary offered. To them, a talent is worth exactly what he or she is paid—no more, no less. There are no norms, no standards, no caps. In that sense anchors are part of a star system similar to those in sports or Hollywood. It is no accident that almost all anchors employ agents and lawyers to protect them from the vagaries of what is a very insecure business.

One of the anchors on WJZ-TV is Denise Koch (III [01:34]). She coanchors the 6:00 and 11:00 p.m. news with Al Sanders (III [11:23]) for the rest of the Eyewitness News Team. She has been in the news business for twelve years, but she did not enter television journalism by the usual paths. She majored in theater rather than communications, acquiring a master's degree. While working as an actress, she was offered a freelance position at WJZ to do segments for "Evening Magazine." From there, she began doing field reporting, and eventually assumed the anchor's chair.

Her daily anchoring of the newscasts begins when she enters the newsroom around 3:00 p.m. each day. After opening mail and returning the inevitable phone messages, she and Sanders meet with the producer to discuss the 6:00 p.m. broadcast. They receive the rundown of the show, which by this time (4:00 p.m.) has been mapped out as tightly as possible. Some days she and Sanders may have been reached earlier at home to discuss a particularly thorny aspect of a story, but on a normal day, the anchors get the stories they will be doing at this meeting.

The next task is to coordinate the script with the other writers and the audio and video technicians. Since the anchors write a lot of the core copy for the show, Koch and Sanders usually find themselves at their keyboard after the technical meeting, working on their assigned stories for each "section"—that segment of the newscast from the opening to the first commercial break. For the hour broadcast at 6:00 p.m., there are seven sections (A through G); the 11:00 p.m. show has 5 sections (A through E).

The anchors at WJZ write until 5:45 p.m., before spending a few minutes in front of the mirror, preparing for the lights and cameras. There are no dressing rooms or makeup personnel waiting for them; Koch and Sanders must prepare on their own. The hour-long broadcast keeps them on the set for the entire time, even though there are frequent cutaways and insertions from other sources.

After the evening edition, the anchors must again meet with the producer and newscast director. They appraise the show in terms of what went right, what went wrong. They discuss what stories were covered on the competing stations, what technical problems need fixing, and how things that were missed can be picked up on the late-night edition. After that, they record some teases, or promos, for the 11:00 p.m. news, and break for dinner.

After another meeting with the producer, where Koch and Sanders receive the late-night format and story assignments, the anchors return to their keyboard for another writing stint. How Koch's story is written is entirely her own decision. Later on, if the executive producer wants to change the writing, compromises are in order. However, it is not usually the anchor's place or responsibility to question a particular story's inclusion in the stack or its position in the hierarchy. Koch, like most anchors who have been working in the business for more than a few years, understands the economics of local news on television. She realizes the need for ratings, the need to entertain as well as inform, and the need to sell advertising.

On some days the preparations for the newscast are disrupted by the late-breaking events that force everything to be changed. On the accompanying videotape, the verdict in the case of Rodney King's arresting officers was announced while WJZ was wrapping its 6:00 p.m. broadcast. There had been no advance warning, and there was not enough time to establish a network feed or downlink from a satellite. Decisions had to be made instantly: Should the anchors scrap their rundown completely, and get whatever information possible on the air before 7:00 p.m., or should they wait until 11:00 p.m., when they would have more time to present a cogent package of information?

The decision to wait until the late-night newscast did not make everyone's preparations any easier, because the riots in Los Angeles became more widespread than anyone expected, and the information that poured in from the West Coast was continually changing, and therefore changing the content of the 11:00 p.m. broadcast.

In general, Denise Koch and her coanchor have a healthy degree of independence in handling the broadcast of any particular news item. Since the 1970s female anchors on local, large-market news shows have become more prevalent; but it was not always so. In the past, local and network news anchors were overwhelmingly male, as the prevailing broadcast philosophy mirrored conventional cultural biases. It was considered acceptable for audiences to watch male anchors such as Walter Cronkite and Eric Sevareid grow older before their eyes, but unacceptable to see older women doing so. The reasons for such thinking are diverse. Some cite historical precedent, others assert market-research factoids that audiences are more willing to accept information from an older man, the image of paternal wisdom and virility, than from an older woman. But the appearance of Connie Chung on "CBS Evening News" in 1993 reflects the changes that have occurred locally for years, and foretells the increased visibility of female anchors both nationally and locally. As more female anchors such as Chung on the national level and Koch on the local level are accepted, it is hoped that such cultural prejudices will become extinct.

ASSIGNMENT EDITOR

Donna Miller (II [01:33]) is the assignment editor at WJZ, and she works closely with producer Cronan and executive producer King. Before coming to Baltimore, she worked her way through the hierarchy of positions at eight other television stations. During that time she has seen the basic local news operation change, which has in turn affected the way she performs her duties as assignment editor.

Miller feels that a local news station today has to be more competitive with other local news channels, has to get there first, and must emphasize getting the best visuals on video and going live from the scene as news happens. In past decades it was enough to report on the event, no matter when it took place.

In order for Miller to maintain the urgent pace of news-gathering, she spends many hours each day on the telephones and listening to the police, fire, and emergency frequencies of her radio scanner (II [01:38]).

She must be able not only to discover what is happening, but also to quickly determine the proximity of the event—how close the incident is to the station will help her decide whether or not the coverage will be live on the scene. Miller must also decide what personnel can get there fastest and who is best qualified to handle the job. In essence, working the assignment editor's desk means working under pressure.

Experience makes the job go more smoothly. Miller has learned how to keep track of her field reporters and equipment vans; she knows what frequencies to monitor on her scanner at the best times of day. She has also cultivated contacts at various agencies whom she can call for an edge on information. The benefit of such personal contact has been limited over the last few years as the media has increasingly betrayed or in some other way imperiled sources. When insiders believe they will get in trouble for sharing information with the media, they stop talking. Miller is experiencing this more and more: a community growing not only more media savvy, but also media wary.

Despite this situation, Miller still depends on telephone input from the community for source material on stories. Almost every day there is at least one potential story the station would know nothing about without calls from concerned individuals. This input is, of course, a double-edged sword. For every story of possible significance, there are unfounded reports from individuals who are less than reliable. A good assignment editor must be patient and learn how to separate fact from fantasy. Miller also feels that one should possess a well-rounded education—having a working familiarity with many subject areas—and the ability to write with clarity and precision.

FIELD REPORTER

Melissa Sander (I [02:20]) is a field reporter at WJZ-TV. She worked the night shift, providing stories for the 11:00 p.m. newscast, until May 1993, when her schedule switched to days for the 6:00 p.m. news. She has worked at the station for almost three years but has been in television for more than eleven years—spending more than nine years as an on-air general assignment reporter. Like many reporters in large markets, she worked her way up to WJZ by taking positions at smaller markets and gradually ascending the ladder rung by rung. Such career climbing often forces a reporter to do more than one job—editing and shooting as well as writing. Smaller-market stations often demand such doubling up from their personnel, and it gives the reporter a firmer understanding of the entire process of creating a video package for broadcast.

Field reporting jobs are highly competitive and hard to obtain. Sander sent out countless résumés and letters, knocked on a lot of doors, and aggressively pursued all openings in the industry until someone rewarded her persistence with a job. Her hardnosed approach to the business has helped shape her into a news veteran who has learned from her mistakes as well as her successes. She notes that as a reporter moves to larger and larger markets, he or she frequently relinquishes more and more control—artistic, technical, or editorial—over the material. It is a reality of the industry that seems unavoidable.

Sander's pace is dictated by time constraints set by producers and assignment editors. Therefore, she is often rushed, which is detrimental to the quality of her finished piece. In addition, she occasionally loses time dealing with the availability of interview subjects and the pace of her videographer and video editor. Her producers have final control over what is called producer's completeness, which allows them freedom to add or remove elements from her story.

To Sander, the most important aspect of getting the story

right is maintaining an objective position. This detachment can be difficult when a story ignites strong personal beliefs, convictions, or emotions in the reporter. A good reporter keeps objectivity in mind at all times, and always strives to treat the material as evenhandedly as possible.

The most interesting story, she feels, is often the one that leaves the issue at hand in the lap of the viewer, letting the audience members form their own opinion or verdict. A problem in maintaining this kind of "fairness doctrine philosophy" occurs when Sander obtains video and an interview from a subject representing one side of the story or issue, but the subject representing the opposite point of view refuses to go on camera or be interviewed at all. Viewers tend to remember what they have seen as well as heard, and on a sensitive or questionable issue, that can leave a story lopsided regardless of the reporter's attempt to address the missing viewpoints.

How, then, does the reporter tell the story without slanting it in the direction of the available video? Sander attempts to write her story so that she herself can provide the alternate view—but only after pleading with her subjects that it is in their best interest to say something, to at least appear on video and seem to say something of substance. Many interviewees have become wary of being misquoted or having their words so skillfully edited that, taken out of context, they can mean something quite different than originally intended.

Many times a field reporter is assigned a story with which he or she disagrees or does not feel particularly in synch. Sander notes that her own ideas for a story or slant on a story are sometimes rejected. Many stories she ends up doing on-air are not self-generated. Her personal philosophy concerning what is newsworthy does not always coincide with that of her superiors. Many reporters feel it important to include reaction and opinion from outsiders in local news stories (since neighbors and friends may compromise objectivity); Sander feels it is more important to include the comments of subjects with some influence or direct bearing on the story. She feels that a reporter should not merely point out events that may affect the community, but rather explain how the events will affect the audience.

As a field reporter, Sander attempts to follow her own sense of good television journalism. She believes that her stories must be more than just "radio with pictures." Sander usually writes "to the video," but she believes that independent textual substance must also be present in a good story. Although a good piece of television journalism can be understood even without the sound, subtlety, irony, and humor are instantly lost without audio. The well-produced story allows viewers "to hear about what they are seeing and to see what they are hearing about."

Learning to listen without coloring the input with a pre-planned agenda is also a challenge for all field reporters. Too many times, reporters have preconceived ideas concerning the kind of story they are looking for. If they are responsive to members of the community, to the people steering them onto the news events, they may uncover a larger or more interesting story. Sander believes that a good television news team responds to viewers' feedback, and that listening is the greatest public service any reporter can perform.

The biggest obstacle to good TV reporting is learning to operate within the time constraints. The longest stories are 2 minutes, with most being assigned 1:15 to 1:30 minutes—not much time to ensure the completeness that makes a good story, that leaves the viewer satisfied that he or she has experienced a true beginning, middle, and end. For this reason, Sander believes that no one should rely solely on television news as his or her total information source. Print and television should easily complement one another.

Working on deadline exerts constant pressure on a reporter. Some reporters thrive under stress and use it to give them the boost and edge to create a good story economically. Not surprisingly, reporters on the day shift have more time and access to their subjects and material. Working the evening and night shifts is more demanding because interview subjects or witnesses are less willing to talk when they would rather be on their way home. Many people do not like to be contacted in the evening hours. Because making deadline for the night edition is thus compounded, a diligent field reporter must be as organized as possible.

Organization begins with maximum familiarity with one's videotape. Knowing where particular shots are located on a field tape can speed up the editing process immeasurably. Time normally spent doing mindless tape searches in the edit booth is better spent in creative assembly; maintaining a video log makes this possible. Having a good memory and ear for catchy or significant sound bites is not something that can be taught, but the reporter who possesses these skills is greatly benefited.

Personally, Sander feels the trend toward tabloidization in local news is little more than a fad. She also hopes that the overemphasis on "techno-toys" in the industry does not overshadow the primary intention of television news, which is to gather news as efficiently as possible and tell it to the audience with the greatest amount of clarity and depth. If the day comes when she must carry her own small, handsized camcorder, she believes that the time she devotes to its operation will be valuable time taken from her real reporting duties.

For a field reporter, nothing can ever change the basic reality of the job: get out there and uncover the stories that have the most local interest.

WRITER

As we have already seen, many members of the news team are involved in writing for the broadcast, from the anchors to the producers to the field reporters. In addition, WJZ employs one full-time writer and several writers who work on a quasi-freelance basis. A typical part-time writer for the station will work weekends and at least two or three days/evenings per week.

Writing assignments vary from day to day, whether condensing national news stories for broadcast or rewriting stories when additional information is uncovered at the last minute.

Prospective writers for WJZ take a writing test that requires them to rewrite a news story, giving it a conversational spin. A writer needs to be able to take thirty seconds worth of information and make it interesting, entertaining, and comprehensive. Many writers serve as interns before taking employment, and many aspire to write and produce their own segments or shows.

There are many schools of thought on how to write news for television. Indeed, entire courses are designed around the concept of telling the story for broadcast; an in-depth analysis of how to write is beyond the scope of this book. However, a brief overview of some accepted principles of good writing and a brief examination of the basic ingredients will at least provide the reader with an appreciation of what is required to write a good story.

First, television newswriting is essentially writing for the eye and the ear, that is, as a verbal accompaniment to a collection of visual images. While this may seem obvious, the differences between writing for the ear only (for radio) or the eye only (for print) and TV can be subtle but dramatic—a lesson quickly learned by radio commentators from the 1940s who were forced in the 1950s to transfer their skills to the new medium of television. Some journalists, such as Edward R. Murrow, made the transition seem effortless, but many others never grasped the following differences:

1. Broadcasting the news is a team effort, requiring some standardization of news copy.
2. Broadcast news is ephemeral. The audience cannot go back and review (or reread) a story not clearly presented. Clarity and ease of comprehension are therefore crucial.
3. The writing style for broadcast news must sound like conversation. (Yoakam and Cremer, 198)

Once these differences are understood, the basics for writing for television news are easier to recognize and employ.

Writing short, direct sentences is critical. Long sentences sound choppy and singsong when read aloud. A short simple sentence has impact but does not confuse the viewer by trying to pack too much information into any one phrase.

Using the active voice is a deceptively simple but very effective principle in communicating the immediacy of broadcast news.

After writing any news copy, the writer should take it out for a test drive: read it aloud. Listen carefully to the rhythm of the sentences, the possibility for tongue-twisting phrases, or the yoking together of words that may sound inappropriate or inadvertently humorous.

Avoiding abbreviations and symbols is always a good habit to cultivate. The object of nonpermanent writing is to keep things from being confusing or distracting. Don't employ usage that will wrongly emphasize part of the story.

Be careful with proper names. Don't throw them into a story without warning or introduction, or the audience will likely miss them. A short phrase that gives the person's title or somehow identifies him or her before mentioning the name can very effectively ensure that the audience will recall the name. Give proper names significance or meaning if possible.

On a similar note, numbers should be employed with care. Rounding off numbers is usually better than trying to stun the audience with an overly precise figure that is likely to be forgotten.

As far as punctuation is concerned, commas and ellipses are used for natural and dramatic pauses, which in turn can emphasize specific pieces of information within the story.

The importance of recording direct quotes as accurately as possible seems more than obvious, yet more than one journalist has made the mistake of trying to "improve" upon a subject's quoted remarks by actually *changing* them. Never change quotations.

The final guideline for writing television news is perhaps the most important: Be aware of all the other elements that make up a televised story, and use them. Sound, background, scene-setting, color, motion, editing, mixing, and producing all contribute to a successful story. The writer who is skillful enough to combine these elements into his or her writing will be very successful.

CHIEF ENGINEER

The chief engineer at any television station has an important job: maintaining the signal that the station transmits. Without a reliable signal, there is no broadcast. Richard Seaby, chief engineer at WJZ-TV, is responsible for this and for overseeing a technical operation that runs twenty-four hours a day, day in and day out. Quality control is a top priority because the signal can never be allowed to go off the air. This is Seaby's chief responsibility.

Among other duties and obligations, compliance with all FCC regulations is also a high priority. The federal agency closely monitors the technical quality of all broadcasters. Because WJZ must keep its signal within the boundaries established in the FCC rules, the chief engineer is very concerned with the calibration of all broadcast equipment. He must make certain that all the station's equipment meets the FCC's broadcast standards. When FCC inspectors visit a television station's facilities, the chief engineer must ensure that equipment specifications and proper licensing of technical employees are in order.

Seaby's daily duties have a certain routine, but he must leave room in his schedule to deal with unexpected or irregular tasks. He must plan work schedules; oversee shift assignments; approve equipment purchases, repairs, and upgrades; and meet with other department heads to integrate their activities.

The engineering department at WJZ-TV comprises two divisions: engineering and operations. Seaby oversees the day-to-day activities of these divisions by delegating responsibility and task management to his assistants.

The television transmitter at WJZ-TV is part of a tripartite tower that soars 1,000 feet above Baltimore. The equipment that feeds the transmitting tower is almost entirely self-monitoring. Transmitter parameters can be monitored and adjusted by computer-controlled telemetering equipment.

Engineering maintenance is the area that employs technicians to handle equipment failures, emergency repairs, testing and preventive tasks, new construction, and renovations. Technicians work around the clock to keep everything in working order, and most systems are redundant—that is, if a component fails, there is a second component available to back it up until the first device is repaired or replaced.

The operations schedule must be planned by Seaby's department in advance, but the schedule is always altered or at least fine-tuned. Overtime, sick leave, and other personnel issues must be handled daily. Daily operations must also deal with nonmajor technical glitches that require "fix-ups" or "tweakings" from an engineer or technician—such as tape-playback problems, poor-quality audio, or signal noise. Another aspect of operations is budgetary. The chief engineer must decide what equipment is required, how much to pay for it, and how cost-efficient it will prove to be over the time necessary to depreciate it. The cost of new technology must be compared to the benefits it will bring the station in terms of money saved or extra revenue generated. A tight economy makes this kind of fiscal responsibility another high priority. Operations must also be aware of the quality of the signal being transmitted by competing stations in the Baltimore DMA.

The chief engineer must maintain the highest levels of

quality control at WJZ-TV, to achieve the best sound and pictures possible. Distortion and signal noise are targeted not only through routine testing and preventive maintenance but also through an operations schedule that includes an awareness of corporate standards and government regulations. High quality control contributes to the station's image in the community and is therefore extremely important to all levels of management at WJZ-TV—a station that prides itself on being very community minded.

The chief engineer must not only be a supervisor, planner, and budgetary analyst, but he must also be as creative and imaginative as possible. To do this, Seaby spends a lot of time keeping abreast of the lightning-quick changes in TV technology. Seaby and his staff must read the reams of trade publications chronicling the research and development of new equipment, techniques, media, and operating philosophies. The greater his knowledge of what is available now and in the future, the greater his own chances of being able to anticipate the station's needs.

Fiscal responsibility looms large because of the cost of new technologies. The expense, use, and potential for return on investment must all be factors under consideration by the chief engineer. Fiber optics, the promising new carrier system discussed in the previous chapter, could open up the broadcast arena to ten times as many players—in the neighborhood of 500 channels. Seaby likens the situation to heading at high speed toward a wall: the wall is the finite amount of money available to establish programming and advertising on all the television channels being made available.

There simply are not enough resources or even product to fill all those channels, and not enough people to make them all attractive shares for commercial investment. Seaby believes that there will be an industry-wide shakeout when many stations—both new and established—will fail because of a non-Euclidean kind of irony: they had too much room to play. When one estimates the incredible costs involved to bring the local news to the public every day, employing a staff of more than seventy people, it would not be surprising to see local television news dwindle and die out.

If the future does bring yet more stations (and therefore less revenues), such as local and regional cable broadcasts competing for the news audience, then the costs of gathering and delivering the news must become a prime consideration. Local broadcast news appears to be standing at the threshold to a new era of technology and advanced communications.

The future of the local news industry and of television itself depends on its leaders' ability to comprehend the words of Newton N. Minow: "A new generation now has the chance to put the vision back into television, to travel from the wasteland to the promised land, and to make television a saving radiance in the sky."

11:00 p.m.
Local News

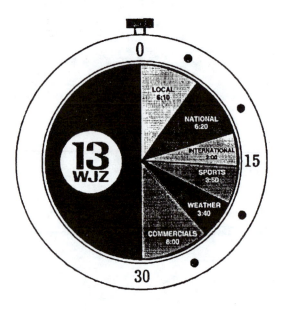

30:00-Minute
Breakdown

APPENDIX 1

Annotated Script and Viewer's Guide to Behind the Scenes at the Local News Videotape

Note: Each of the first four sections of this video is accompanied by a running clock to help identify the participants and equipment referred to throughout Chapters 4 and 5. The reader is strongly urged to reference the Newscast Production Materials found in Appendix 2 while viewing the section of the videotape called Part Four: Studio News Production.

PART ONE: ENG Package Production

1. (0:00)
IT'S 3:30 PM . . . THE 11 O'CLOCK PRODUCER, AS-SIGNMENT EDITOR, AND REPORTER MEET TO DISCUSS WHAT'S ON TAP FOR TONIGHT. THE DAYTIME ASSIGN-MENT EDITOR BRIEFS THEM ON A POSSIBLE STORY. (NATURAL SOUND)

Producer Margaret Cronan appears in the ADO effect (showing "ENG Package Production" title) with Reporter Melissa Sander. As the running clock appears in the lower right-hand corner of the screen, Evening Assignment Editor Donna Miller appears in full-screen. Profiles of each individual appear in Chapter 5.

2. (0:26)
MEANTIME, PHOTOGRAPHER MIKE CORKRAN GEARS UP FOR THE NIGHT AHEAD ... LOADING HIS VAN WITH THE NECESSARY EQUIPMENT. (:04)

Corkran's ENG equipment includes a Betacam camcorder, battery belt, auxiliary lighting pack, cables and connectors, and a variety of microphones, including a handheld cardioid mic for the reporter. The van carries video-playback and microwave-transmission equipment.

3. (0:33)
REPORTER MELISSA SANDER NOW MAKES CALLS FOR HER STORY ON A LOCAL RECREATION CENTER IN A NEIGHBORHOOD PLAGUED BY CRIME. THE CENTER MAY LOSE THE POLICE OFFICERS WHO RUN IT BECAUSE OF CITY BUDGET CUTS. (:08)

This story illustrates several principles discussed in Chapter 3: newsworthiness, interest, and possible future impact. Reinforcing the need for good visuals, the chase scene that ensues was not only fortuitous, but also demonstrative.

4. (0:48)
AS MELISSA MAKES MORE CALLS, A DAYSIDE REPORTER WRITES HER STORY ON THE COMPUTER.

5. (1:32)
MELISSA AND MIKE HEAD OUT ... MELISSA HELPS MIKE WITH DIRECTIONS AND BRIEFS HIM ON THEIR STORY.

6. (1:56)
THEY ARRIVE ON THE SCENE ... MIKE WHITE-BALANCES HIS CAMERA: USING A WHITE SHEET OF PAPER, HE SETS THE CAMERA TO REGISTER ALL COLORS PROPERLY. IF A CAMERA HASN'T BEEN WHITE-BALANCED, VIDEO MAY APPEAR BLUE, ORANGE, OR GREEN.

7. (2:45)
SUDDENLY, A POLICE OFFICER CHASES A YOUNG
MAN UP A NEARBY HILL . . . MELISSA AND MIKE FOLLOW.
MIKE MAKES SURE TO GET IT ALL ON TAPE.

7A. (3:36)
THE OFFICER FINDS A GUN . . .

8. (4:37)
ONCE THE OFFICER GETS THE YOUNG MAN INSIDE
THE REC. CENTER, MELISSA LISTENS IN AS THE POLICE
TRY TO FIND OUT EXACTLY WHAT HAPPENED . . . AP-
PARENTLY A CHILD HAD REPORTED SOME TYPE OF
DRUG DEAL GOING ON UP THE HILL . . . THE YOUNG MAN
THE OFFICER CHASED WAS FIRST THOUGHT TO BE A
SUSPECT, BUT POLICE QUICKLY DETERMINE THAT HE'S
ACTUALLY THE VICTIM: TWO MEN HAD POINTED THE
LOADED GUN AT THE YOUNG MAN AND DEMANDED HIS
SNEAKERS . . . FOR SOME REASON THE MEN FLED . . .
BUT DROPPED THEIR GUN.

9. (4:57)
ALREADY KNOWING THAT SHE'LL USE THE AT-
TEMPTED ROBBERY INCIDENT IN HER STORY, MELISSA
SETS OUT TO BUILD THE REST OF HER PACKAGE, IN-
TRODUCING THE PHOTOGRAPHER, MIKE, TO THE PO-
LICE OFFICER SHE'LL NEED TO INTERVIEW.

9A (5:09)
MELISSA NOW GETS A CHANCE TO INTERVIEW THE
YOUNG MAN . . . PERHAPS HIS STORY WILL
STRENGTHEN THE FIGHT TO KEEP THE OFFICERS AT
THE REC. CENTER.

10. (5:57)
MELISSA CONDUCTS A SUCCESSFUL INTERVIEW . . .
LEARNING WHY POLICE OFFICERS FEEL IT'S NECES-
SARY FOR THEM TO BE PART OF THE REC. CENTER . . .
THEY SAY KIDS NEED TO BE NURTURED INSIDE AND

OUTSIDE THE HOME AND NEED TO KNOW THAT THE POLICE ARE THERE TO HELP.

11. (6:33)
MIKE SHOOTS COVER VIDEO, OR B-ROLL, INSIDE THE REC. CENTER. MELISSA WILL CHOOSE THE BEST SHOTS TO COMPLEMENT HER INTERVIEWS AND RE-PORTER AUDIO.

In creating the package and to ensure continuity editing, it is necessary to have cutaways, called B-roll (a term borrowed from the film era). This enables the reporter to tell the story seamlessly.

11A. (7:07)
MELISSA SEES AN OPPORTUNITY FOR VIDEO SHE MAY NEED IN HER PACKAGE. SHE TELLS MIKE WHAT SHE'S LOOKING FOR.

12. (7:33)
OUTSIDE MELISSA TALKS TO SEVERAL CHILDREN ABOUT THE POSSIBILITY OF LOSING THE OFFICERS WHO RUN THEIR REC. CENTER.

13. (3:13)
BACK INSIDE MELISSA AND MIKE LOOK FOR MORE KIDS TO TALK TO . . . SHE FINDS OUT WHAT IT'S LIKE TO GROW UP IN A CRIME-RIDDEN NEIGHBORHOOD. KIDS TELL HER WHY THEY NEED THE REC. CENTER AND THE POLICE WHO RUN IT . . . MELISSA LEARNS THAT THE KIDS CONSIDER THE OFFICERS THEIR FRIENDS AND COUNT ON THEM FOR PROTECTION.

As Sander stated in Chapter 5, one of the most important aspects of getting the story is to maintain an objective position, as evidenced in her methods during this scene.

14. (8:42)
ONCE THE SHOOT IS COMPLETE, THE CREW TAKES A LOOK AT THE TAPES ON THE MONITORS IN THE VAN.

15. (9:24)

THE CREW IS NOW AT A SECOND LOCATION . . . HERE THEY INTERVIEW A BALTIMORE CITY COUNCILMAN WHO GREW UP WITH A REC. CENTER IN HIS NEIGHBORHOOD. WHEN HE WAS YOUNG, HE PARTICIPATED IN POLICE ATHLETIC LEAGUE EVENTS. TONIGHT HE'S FIGHTING TO KEEP THE REC. CENTERS OPEN AND RUNNING WITH POLICE ASSISTANCE. THOUGH ULTIMATELY HIS SOUND BITES DON'T MAKE IT INTO MELISSA'S FINISHED PACKAGE, SHE USES MUCH OF THE INFORMATION.

Sander exhibits the proper miking technique by allowing the subject to speak over the top of the mic, and never handing it to the subject. The photographer exhibits proper camera technique by tucking in his elbow to create the stability of a tripod, while determining the correct focal point.

PART TWO: ENG Image Processing

1. (0:00)

BACK AT THE NEWSROOM, MELISSA TAKES A SEAT AT A VIEWING STATION AND BEGINS LOGGING HER TAPES . . . SINCE EACH TAPE IS TIME-CODED, SHE CAN WRITE DOWN THE EXACT TIMES OF SHOTS SHE MAY USE, SO THAT ONCE SHE'S IN THE EDITING ROOM, SHE AND THE EDITOR CAN QUICKLY LOCATE NECESSARY VIDEO AND SOUND BITES. THE SOUND BITES MELISSA SELECTS WILL BE THE MOST CONCISE SHE CAN FIND TO TELL HER STORY . . . TOTAL RUNNING TIME OF HER PACKAGE WILL BE NO MORE THAN ONE MINUTE AND 45 SECONDS. WHEN CHOOSING BITES, SHE TIMES THEM OUT TO THE SECOND SO THAT WHEN SHE WRITES, SHE KNOWS HOW MUCH COPY, OR REPORTER TRACK, SHE CAN USE WITH THE BITES WITHOUT GOING OVER HER ALLOTTED TIME.

Sander logs her tapes on a Betacam deck; the headphones plugged into a jack on the deck allow her to work without disturbing others in the newsroom.

2. (1:27)
AROUND THE NEWSROOM, THE REST OF THE 11 O'CLOCK STAFF PREPARES FOR THE SHOW. DONNA MILLER, THE NIGHT ASSIGNMENT EDITOR, MONITORS THE SCANNERS FOR BREAKING NEWS.

(1:50)
NEWSCAST DIRECTOR GUY RAYMOND ORGANIZES HIS PAPERWORK.

The rundown, script, and Chyron/ENG sheets used by Raymond appear in Appendix 2.

(2:04)
PRODUCER MARGARET CRONAN READS WIRE COPY STORED IN THE COMPUTER AND KEEPS AN EYE ON THE NETWORK FEED COMING DOWN ON A NEARBY MONITOR.

The computer used by Cronan is part of the BASYS Newsdesk computer system decsribed in Chapter 4.

3. (2:26)
A CHYRON OPERATOR TYPES NAMES AND NUMBERS INTO THE MEMORY OF THIS VIDEO WORD PROCESSOR, CALLED A CHARACTER GENERATOR (CG). IT IS NAMED CHYRON AFTER THE EQUIPMENT MANUFACTURER WITH THE MOST ESTABLISHED BRAND NAME. THE CHYRON ALLOWS FOR VECTOR FONTS THAT CAN BE SCALED TO DIFFERENT TYPE SIZES. IN THE CG VOCABULARY, TYPEFACES ARE CALLED FONTS. THESE TITLE GRAPHICS WILL BE USED DURING THE SHOW, CALLED UP LIVE FROM A FLOPPY DISK, AS A SOUND BITE APPEARS ON THE SCREEN, OR AS A SPORTSCASTER CALLS FOR A SCORE.

4. (2:56)

IN THE NEWSROOM, WRITERS WORK ON STORIES AND CONTINUE TO GATHER INFORMATION TO BE USED IN THE SHOW.

5. (3:09)

IN THE ART DEPARTMENT, DAN WIG USES A SPECIAL GRAPHICS GENERATOR CALLED A PAINT BOX, THE TRADE NAME OF A MACHINE MANUFACTURED BY THE QUANTEL CORPORATION. HE USES A STYLUS, OR ELEC-TRONIC PEN, AND A TABLE (A BLOCK WITH A FLAT SURFACE SENSITIVE TO THE STYLUS). THE STYLUS IS THE BRUSH. DRAWING WITH THE STYLUS PRODUCES A CORRESPONDING DRAWING ON THE SCREEN. THE STY-LUS IS PRESSURE SENSITIVE: THE HARDER ONE PUSHES THE THICKER THE IMAGE. A STROKE TO ANY EDGE OF THE TABLET OVERLAYS THE IMAGE WITH A MENU SYSTEM THAT MIMICS A PAINTER'S PALETTE. ASSOCIATED WITH THE PALETTE IS A MENU OF OP-TIONS TO DETERMINE THE CHARACTERISTICS OF THE BRUSH. BRUSHES CAN BE SELECTED IN VARIOUS SIZES, OFTEN AS SMALL AS A SINGLE PIXEL, AND ALLOW ENLARGEMENTS OF TWO AND FOUR TIMES THE SIZE OF THE IMAGE TO PERMIT WORK ON DETAILS. BRUSHES IMITATE OIL PAINT, WATERCOLOR, OR AIRBRUSH AND ALLOW POINT-TO-POINT LINE CONNECTION. ANOTHER MENU OFFERS STENCIL CAPABILITIES AND ALLOWS DAN TO COPY AN OBJECT AS A PASTE-UP AND KEY IT OVER A BACKGROUND. THE PAINT BOX IS A 30-FRAME-PER-SECOND REAL-TIME SYSTEM, CAPTURING A FRAME OF MOVING VIDEO FASTER THAN 1/30TH OF A SECOND, THE DURATION OF ONE VIDEO FRAME. AS YOU CAN SEE, THE PAINT BOX WAS DESIGNED FOR ARTISTS, NOT COMPUTER PROGRAMMERS. DAN IS BUILDING WHAT IS CALLED A VIOLATOR FOR THE SHOW'S TOP STORY. DURING THE SHOW, THE NEWSCAST DIRECTOR WILL CALL FOR A VIOLATOR AT THE BEGINNING OF THE FIRST STORY . . . IT WILL THEN APPEAR TO FLY OFF THE SCREEN AFTER A FEW SECONDS. THE VIOLATOR IS

USED TO SET THE TOP STORY APART FROM THE REST OF THE SHOW.

6. (5:27)
BACK IN EDITING, THE SPORTS PRODUCER BEGINS EDITING TONIGHT'S SPORTSCAST.

7. (6:21)
IN THE SPORTS OFFICE, SPORTSCASTER JOHN BUREN ALSO BEGINS PREPARATIONS FOR TONIGHT'S SHOW.

PART THREE: *Studio News Preproduction*

Producer Cronan is seen in the ADO to introduce Part Three with Al Sanders, coanchor of the 11:00 p.m. news.

1. (0:01)
LATE IN THE AFTERNOON, FOUR LOS ANGELES POLICE OFFICERS ARE ACQUITTED IN THE BEATING OF RODNEY KING . . . THAT NIGHT, LOS ANGELES GOES UP IN FLAMES.

2. (0:09)
THE NIGHT TEAM GETS TO WORK TRYING TO BRING THE L.A. STORY HOME TO BALTIMORE . . . ANCHOR AL SANDERS AND PRODUCER MARGARET CRONAN MEET TO DISCUSS THE LEAD PACKAGE: AN OVERALL LOOK AT THE ACQUITTAL AND ITS EFFECTS ON THE PEOPLE OF LOS ANGELES. AL USES NETWORK FOOTAGE AND SOUND BITES TO BUILD THE STORY. BOTH THE PRODUCER AND EXECUTIVE PRODUCER KEEP THEIR EYES ON THE NETWORK FEEDS, ALERTING ALL TO ANY USABLE VIDEO. (:21)

Although the lead story is national in scope, it is of extreme local interest because of the possible future impact on the community, especially in a city like Baltimore that has a large African-American population. This is one of the most important principles of local newsgathering. Other principles evident are timeliness, interest, and potential for controversy.

3. (1:33)

ANCHOR DENISE KOCH AWAITS LOCAL VIDEO AND REACTION, BEING SHOT BY EYEWITNESS NEWS CREWS. HER PACKAGE WILL DEMONSTRATE HOW BALTIMOREANS FEEL ABOUT AN EXPLOSIVE SITUATION THOUSANDS OF MILES AWAY. (:11)

4. (2:03)

DENISE NOW HAS SOME OF HER REACT BITES BACK IN-HOUSE . . . SHE'LL LOG WHAT SHE HAS AND WILL START BUILDING HER PACKAGE WHILE AWAITING MORE BITES BEING GATHERED BY OTHER REPORTERS AND PRODUCERS IN THE FIELD.

5. (2:25)

THE PRODUCERS, ANCHORS, AND OTHER NIGHT TEAM MEMBERS GATHER AROUND THE NETWORK FEED MONITORS, WATCHING AS THE STORY CONTINUES TO UNFOLD, LOOKING FOR THE BEST VIDEO. (:09)

This scene reinforces the idea that television writing involves "writing to the video" and emphasizes the techniques necessary to tell the story with visuals.

6. (3:11)

KNOWING WHAT B-ROLL HE'LL HAVE TO USE WITH THE LOS ANGELES "OFFICIAL" SOUND BITES HE'S CHOSEN, AL HEADS TO HIS OFFICE TO WRITE.

7. (4:18)

THE NIGHT WRITER FINISHES UP OTHER PARTS OF THE SHOW AS THE ANCHORS WORK ON THEIR PACKAGES.

8. (4:30)

THE PRODUCER LEARNS SHE HAS THE OPTION OF

A NETWORK LIVE SHOT AT THE TOP OF THE SHOW. (:03)

9. (5:37)
FIELD PRODUCER AND NIGHT WRITER MITCH FRIED-MAN HAD GONE TO BALTIMORE–WASHINGTON INTER-NATIONAL AIRPORT TO INTERVIEW MARYLANDERS JUST RETURNING FROM LOS ANGELES . . . NONE HAD KNOWN ABOUT THE VERDICT OR THE RIOTS. THE NEWS HAD BROKEN DURING THE FLIGHT BACK FROM CALI-FORNIA. MITCH EXPLAINS TO DENISE WHAT SOUND BITES SHE MAY WANT TO USE AS PART OF HER LOCAL REACT PACKAGE. (:20)

10. (6:58)
EDITORS TIE UP AS MANY LOOSE ENDS AS POSSI-BLE WHILE AWAITING THE LAST-MINUTE EDITING CRUNCH, A SURE THING ON SUCH A BUSY NIGHT. (:05)

11. (7:18)
AS THE ANCHORS, PRODUCERS, AND EDITORS CO-ORDINATE THE LOS ANGELES STORY, THE NIGHT TEAM REPORTERS CONTINUE THEIR WORK ON OTHER NEWS OF THE DAY. MELISSA SANDER WRITES HER STORY ON THE CLOSING OF THE REC. CENTER. (:12)

12. (7:41)
AS 11 O'CLOCK APPROACHES, DENISE EDITS HER PACKAGE.

13. (8:39)
IN ANOTHER BOOTH, MELISSA AND ANOTHER EDI-TOR BEGIN PIECING TOGETHER HER POLICE REC. CEN-TER STORY, STILL AN IMPORTANT ELEMENT IN THE SHOW.

14. (9:02)-AFTER "NORMAL"
DESPITE THE SERIOUSNESS OF THE DAY'S EVENTS, PEOPLE STILL WANT TO KNOW WHETHER IT'S GOING TO RAIN OR SHINE TOMORROW. WEATHERPERSON BOB

TURK PUTS TOGETHER HIS FORECAST IN THE WEATHER CENTER. HE UPDATES MAPS THAT HAVE CHANGED SINCE THE EARLY NEWSCAST. HE ALSO ACCESSES NATIONAL RADAR THROUGH A SATELLITE DOWNLINK AND COMPUTER DISK PROVIDED BY KAVOURAS, A PRIVATE WEATHER SERVICE THE STATION SUBSCRIBES TO. BOB CREATES AN ANIMATION LOOP SHOWING NATIONAL WEATHER TRENDS AND BUILDS HIS OWN FORECAST MAP USING INFORMATION FROM THE NATIONAL WEATHER SERVICE AND ACCU-WEATHER. HIS ACTUAL ON-AIR PRESENTATION IS AN AD-LIB SEGMENT . . . HE USES A WIRELESS MICRO-PHONE AND NO SCRIPT. (:34)

15. (11:17)
IN THE NEWSROOM, THE PRODUCER WATCHES THE NETWORK FEEDS FOR ANY LATE-BREAKING VIDEO OR SOUND.

16. (11:29)
ANCHORMAN AL SANDERS TRACKS THE AUDIO PORTION OF "WORLD WRAP," A CAPSULIZED LOOK AT THE MAJOR NATIONAL AND INTERNATIONAL NEWS OF THE DAY. THE ANCHOR'S AUDIO AND THE VIDEO OF EACH "WORLD WRAP" STORY ARE THEN TAKEN TO POSTPRODUCTION.

17. (12:02)
IN POSTPRODUCTION . . . A SPECIAL EDITOR USES A COMPUTERIZED EDITING FACILITY TO FORM THE "DAY IN REVIEW" AND "WORLD WRAP" SEGMENTS. WITH VIDEO, ANCHOR AUDIO, ANIMATION, AND SPECIAL EFFECTS AT HER DISPOSAL, SHE BUILDS TWO ENCAPSU-LATED SEGMENTS, ONE CONTAINING THE LOCAL NEWS OF THE DAY, THE OTHER, NATIONAL AND INTERNA-TIONAL STORIES.

PART FOUR: Studio News Production

During this segment of the videotape, the actual on-air newscast, as seen by the viewing public, appears in the lower left-hand quadrant. This effect is a good example of the use of an ADO. Also note that during this section, you are hearing the newscast director's "private line" to the entire crew, mixed with the actual on-air audio.

Note: A commercial break occurs on the running clock at 12:47 with a fade to black. The program continues with the running clock at 14:30.

1. (AL AND DENISE HEADING DOWN HALL AFTER SHOW)
AFTER THE NEWSCAST, THE ANCHORS HEAD BACK TO THE NEWSROOM FOR THE POSTSHOW MEETING.

2. (SHOT OF MARGARET GOING OVER LOG)
THE ASSIGNMENT EDITOR HAS COMPILED A LOG, LISTING WHAT STORIES THE COMPETITORS COVERED. NIGHT TEAM MEMBERS DISCUSS THE LOG, COMPARING THE OTHER SHOWS TO THEIR OWN. (NATURAL SOUND)

3. (HELENE CLAPPING)
THE EXECUTIVE PRODUCER OFFERS CONGRATULATIONS ON A JOB WELL DONE.

4. EVERYONE STANDS UP AND HEADS FOR HOME.

APPENDIX 2

Newscast Production Materials:
An Annotated Guide

This guide has several sections:

Section One: The rundown (with the newscast director's personal annotations)

Section Two: The still-store log

Section Three: The newscast script and Chyron/ENG sheets (with the newscast director's personal annotations). The author's annotations for the newscast script appear at the bottom of each page.

The following list is a key to the newscast director's personal shorthand that appears throughout these materials. (For further clarification, see Glossary.)

Numbers 1, 2, & 3 = Cameras in the studio

Numbers ①, ②, & ③ = Camera bust shots

Symbols 1^7, 2^7, & 3^7 = Over-the-shoulder (OTS) graphics

Symbols 1_x, 2_x, & 3_x = 2-shot on camera

Symbols 1_{xx}, 2_{xx}, & 3_{xx} = 3-shot on camera

Symbol 1ck = camera 1 chromakey (Section Three, page 9)

Symbol 1A = camera 1 with Ampex Digital Optics (ADO), over-the-shoulder scores (see sports in Section Three)

Symbol 1_x^{c6} = 2-shot on camera 1 with camera 6 in effects (EFX)

Symbol $\lceil$8/21 = insert violator (still-store 8 keyed over VT machine #21)

Symbol / = a wipe; a transition between video sources

Section One:

The Rundown (see facing page)

The titles at the top of each column of the rundown are explained as follows:

Page = page # of Section Three

TAL = talent (Denise Koch [DK]; Al Sanders [AS]; both [D/A]; John Buren, sports [JB]; Bob Turk, weather [BT]; All [entire cast of talent])

SLUG-RPT = the content of the noted page of script in Section Three

EFFEX = indicates choice of camera shot and type of effect

VID = video source (e.g., ENG, chromakey, or SS [still-store])

AUD = type of audio (e.g., voiceover [VO], sound-on-tape [SOT])

COPY = the amount of time the written copy is anticipated to run

SOT = sound-on-tape; used to determine the amount of time the package is anticipated to run.

BKTIME = backtime; the point where the producer is in real-time relative to the running time of the show. Theoretically backtime should begin at 0:00. Please note that the rundown begins at 0:33, which means that the show was 33 seconds heavy and the producer must adjust the newscast to remove this extra time.

DIRECTOR = first line indicates producer's name; second line is the newscast director (not to be confused with the news director of the entire department); lines following are personal annotations of the newscast director for tape machines and other specialized graphics, such as Chyron.

```
   raymond              Wed Apr 29 22:16  page   1
PAGE   TAL SLUG:RPT           EFFEX   VID   AUD    COPY SOT  EK TIME DIRECTOR
```

PAGE	TAL	SLUG:RPT	EFFEX	VID	AUD	COPY	SOT	EK TIME	DIRECTOR
						0:00		0:33	PROD:CRONAN
						0:00		0:33	DIR:RAYMOND
*****	****	**11PM NEWS 4/29/92*	***	*****	*****	0:00	0:00	0:33	***1******
*****	****	*NEWS (OPEN**********	*****	VTR**	**stee	0:00	0:56	0:33	52
0E	A/D	HELLO	2SHOT			0:06	0:00	1:29	2x
0C	AS	INTRO L-A LIVE	BUSY			0:10	0:00	1:36	22
03A	??	LOS ANGELES LIVE	MICRO		SOT	2:00		1:46 27	23
0BD	AS	TAG/VERDICT	BUSY	ENG	SOT	0:10	1:30	3:46	20
4	A/D	TAG/2SHOT	2SHOT			0:06	0:00	5:25	2 / Z1
4B	DK	BALTIMORE REACTS	SS	VIDEO	SOT	0:07	1:30	6:31 /7	
07	DAR	TAG/2SHOT				0:10	0:00	7:08	
8	AS	MIDTOWN POLO	MS BUST	ENG	SOT	0:10	1:45	7:18	22
9	AS	TAG	TAG			0:05	0:00	9:13	
0F	DK	MAKE-UP WEATHER	BUST	C-KEY BOB		0:20		9:18	kc
10	DK	DAY IN REVIEW	SS	ENG	SOT/SS	0:10	1:00	9:38 27	23
11	AS	SHADOW DAY	DEBS BUST	ENG	SOT	0:13	1:52	10:48	20
12	AS	TAG	BUST			0:03	0:00	12:53	
13	D/A	S-TEASE SPORTS	2SHOT	EFFEX JOHN		0:30		12:56	C6
13A	D/A	S-TEASE NEWS:AMTRAK	2SHOT	ENG	VO	0:00	0:00	13:26 2x	21
13B	D/A	S-TEASE NEWS:SHIPS	WIPE	ENG	VO	0:00		13:26	22
*****	****	**SPOTS 1**********	*****	*****	*****	0:00	2:00	13:26	
21	ALL	WEATHER	3SHOT			0:00	3:00	16:26	
						0:00	0:00	18:26	
22	A/D	NEWS TEASE:PLANE	2shot	ENG	VO	0:10	0:00	18:26 2x	20
*****	****	**SPOTS 2**********	*****	*****	*****	0:00	2:15	18:36	
		**** LOTTERY ****				0:00		20:51	
31	DK	PLANE IN BAY	BUST	ENG	VO	0:17		20:51	20
32	D/A	2SHOT	2SHOT			0:10	0:00	21:08 2x	
33	AS	WORLD WRAP	SS	ENG	SOT/BU	0:10	0:45	21:18 3 7	21
34	DK	BAND BENEFIT	BUST	ENG	VO	0:17		22:13	22
36	A/DJ	TEASE/SPORTS SCORES	2SHOT	VT/CY	VO	0:40	0:00	22:30 2x	7/2
*****	****	**SPOTS 3**********	*****	*****	*****	0:00	2:10	23:10	
41	ALL	--SPORTS11--	3SHOT			0:00	0:20	26:20	
A	J6	ORIOLES MINNESOTA	BUST	ENG	VO	0:55	0:00	26:40	20
B	J6	WILD:AH	BUST	ENG	VO	0:25	0:00	26:35	21
C	J6	CAPS PENS	BUST	ENG	VO	0:35	0:00	27:00	22
D	J6	NBA SCORES BOX	DSS			0:15	0:00	27:35	
E	J6	BULLS HEAT	COLD	ENG	VO	0:20	0:00	27:50	23
F	J6	HOPKINS LACROSSE	BUST	ENG	VO	0:25	0:00	28:10	20
G	J6					0:00	0:00	28:35	
H	J6					0:00	0:00	28:35	
42	BJ	AROUND TOWN	3SHOT	C-KEY		0:30	0:00	28:35 2x	kc
43	AS	COUNTRY MUSIC AWARDS	BUST	ENG	VO	0:25	0:00	29:05	21
44	ALL	BYE/CREDITS-DR 27:16 3SHOT C-FAT 28:15				0:10	0:20	29:30	

```
              —WORTH-HEINEMANN
```

Section Two:

Still-Store Log (see facing page)

This page is provided for both the newscast director and the technical director (the switcher), so that he or she can load the still-stores in the sequence of the show.

The notation FEED BARS AND TONE TO QUAD means that the technical director should send color bars and a 1-kHz tone to the tape room (the Quad) so that the VTR operator can set up a tape for the repeat telecast later the next morning.

Titles of columns are as follows:

SLUG = the number of the page in the script of Section Three

STILL STORE = the title of the page associated with the image to be called up by the newscast director. The number and letter code following the title refer to address, or location, where the computer can find the stored image. For example, on page 3, the notation 9-11 is the top story's address in the computer, and F/S-F/X means Full-Screen Effects. The line below page 3 has no page designation; this is called CLEAR CLUTCH, which means that a page of black must appear between a full-screen still-store and an over-the-shoulder still-store. On page 5, BALT REAX is Baltimore's reaction to the Rodney King civil disturbance, which is stored at 9-12B (screen right); in addition, camera 1 and the violator for SS 9-13 are again in full-screen effects (F/S-F/X). Letter A stands for a screen-right graphic; letter B for a screen-left graphic.

```
   raymond                Wed Apr 29 22:13  page   1

SLUG                      ANCHOR    WRITER                        STATUS TIME
11:00 STILL STONE                   raymond  4/29                 HOLD   0:01
================================================================================
        11:00 STILL STONE

        FEED BARS & TONE TO QUAD

3     TOP STORY NIDON         911-F/S-F/X
      -= CLEAR CLUTCH =-       0000-F/S
5     BALT RELAX OTS          912-B [CAM-1]
5     BALT RELAX VIO.         913-F/S-F/X
      -= CLEAR CLUTCH =-       0000-F/S
10    DAY IN REVIEW           7124-B [CAM-2]
9     WAKE UP FORECAST        920-F.S.          << 7321 S/S -0- CHROMA KEY
1X    SUPER TZ SPRTS FRAME:   7014-F/S
* * * * * SPOTS * * * * * * * * * *
2X    WEX CURR-(IDE)          992-993-F/S       << 7359-7360
2X    WEX STAX                10-19-F.S.
2x    TONIGHT/TOMORROE        994-995-F/S       << 7361-7362
2X    5/DAY FORECAST          20-F/S.           << 7305
* * * * * SPOTS * * * * * * * * *
$ $ $ $ $ LOTTERY $ $ $ $ 998-F.S.             >>>  7139
$ $ $ BUBBA NUMBERS $ $ $ 999-F.S.             >>>  ONLY ONNA FEW O.^ S
      -= CLEAR CLUTCH =-       0000-F/S
33    WORLD WRAP              7194-A [CAM-3]
* * * * * SPOTS * * * * * * * * * *
-C    HOOP BOX SCORZ          7514-F/S-B-1
4X    AROUND DA TOWN          7340-F/S          <<<<7340-7341-7341
     ^   ^   ^   ^   ^   ^   ^   ^   ^   ^   ^   ^   ^   ^   ^   ^   ^   ^   ^   ^
  ^   ^   ^   ^   ^   ^   ^   ^   ^   ^   ^   ^   ^   ^   ^   ^   ^   ^   ^   ^
```

Section Three: Newscast Script

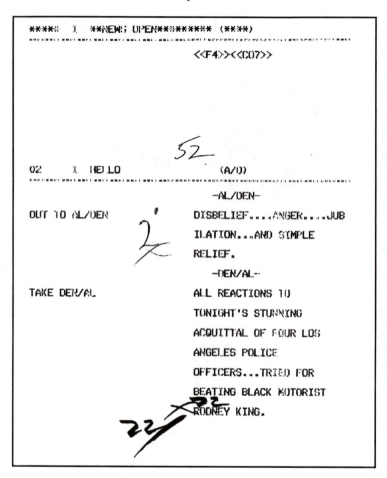

Page 1 Indicates the number of the tape machine (#52) that contains the preproduced opening segment that is repeated every night.

Page 2 Personal annotation for a 2-shot of Al and Denise. The "22" designation indicates the tape machine (#22) for accompanying video images.

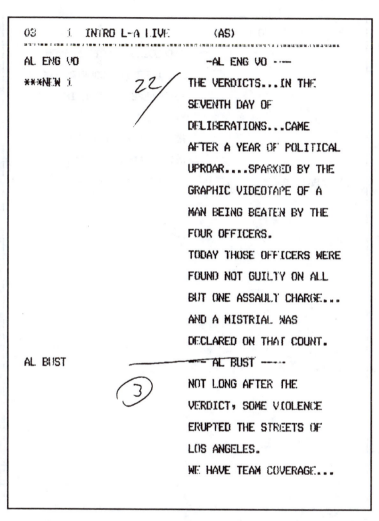

```
03      1   INTRO L-A LIVE        (AS)

AL ENG VO                     -AL ENG VO -—
***NEW 1                22/   THE VERDICTS...IN THE
                              SEVENTH DAY OF
                              DELIBERATIONS...CAME
                              AFTER A YEAR OF POLITICAL
                              UPROAR....SPARKED BY THE
                              GRAPHIC VIDEOTAPE OF A
                              MAN BEING BEATEN BY THE
                              FOUR OFFICERS.
                              TODAY THOSE OFFICERS WERE
                              FOUND NOT GUILTY ON ALL
                              BUT ONE ASSAULT CHARGE...
                              AND A MISTRIAL WAS
                              DECLARED ON THAT COUNT.
AL BUST         ————————— AL BUST —--
                  (3)         NOT LONG AFTER THE
                              VERDICT, SOME VIOLENCE
                              ERUPTED THE STREETS OF
                              LOS ANGELES.
                              WE HAVE TEAM COVERAGE...
```

Page 3 Indicates a bust shot of Al on camera 3; VT 22 continues to roll. The #27 indicates that the live report will be found on router #27. Live shots must be sent through routers to synch them up so they can be genlocked.

```
03      2   INTRO L-A LIVE

                          INCLUDING REACTION FROM
                          ALL OVER THE COUNTRY AND
                          FROM HERE AT HOME IN
                          MARYLAND.
                          WE BEGIN WITH A LIVE
                          REPORT FROM CALIFORNIA.
LIVE SAT UP               --- LIVE SAT UP ---

                          27
```

Page 3A (Script sheet) This is a sheet for the router that contains a personal annotation to indicate the ABC network feed roll cue. The notation 1:49 is the amount of time that the live ABC commentator in Los Angeles remained silent while the station ran a prepackaged video report (sent earlier from the network) on the disturbances. This same footage was rolled in by all local ABC affiliates nationwide who aired the live report and took the "live feed."

REPORTER/WRITER _____ PAGE _3A_

CHYRON/ENG SHEET

| | 6:30AM | NOON | 6:00PM | 11:00PM | OTHER |

DATE: _____

EDITOR: _Kim_

INSERT - L.A. live shot

TIME	AUDIO	SUPER TIME IN	OUT	CHYRON INFORMATION	CHYRON ADDRESS
30	SOT				
48	SOT			*corrections in the future*	

BLACK TIME: _____

WJZ-TV 13

Page 3A (Chyron/ENG sheet) This designates the insert of the L.A. live shot.

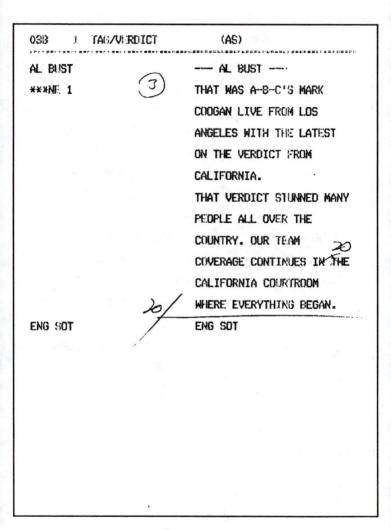

Page 3B (Script sheet) This indicates a bust shot of Al; there is also a sound-on-tape with ENG.

```
04     1   TAG/2SHOT              (A/D)
```

-AL/DENISE 2 SHOT-   -AL/DENISE 2 SHOT-
                                  RODNEY KING'S LAWYER SAYS
                                  HE AND HIS CLIENT ARE
                                  OUTRAGED AT A VERDICT
                                  THAT SENDS A MESSAGE IT'S
                                  O.K. TO BEAT SOMEBODY
                                  WHEN THEY'RE DOWN.
-DENISE/AL 2 SHOT-   -DENISE/AL 2 SHOT-
                                  IN BALTIMORE TONIGHT, THE
                                  HEAD OF THE N-A-A-C-P DR.
                                  BENJAMIN HOOKS IS CALLING
                                  THE VERDICT
                                  'OUTRAGEOUS...A MOCKERY
                                  OF JUSTICE'.
```
```

```
05     1  BALTIMORE REACTS     (DK)
```

-DENISE/SS-   /7   -DENISE/SS-
                                           HOWEVER, DR. HOOKS IS
                                           URGING THE BLACK
                                           COMMUNITY TO USE ITS
                                           ANGER TO TRY AND IMPROVE
                                           RELATIONS BETWEEN
                                           AFRICAN-AMERICANS AND THE
                                           POLICE. THE NAACP'S
                                           EMMETT BURNS IS ALSO
                                           CALLING ON THE BLACK
                                           COMMUNITY TO NOT
                                           REACT...EVEN THOUGH HE
                                           SAYS THE VERDICT TURNS 2/
                                           BACK THE CLOCK 40 YEARS
                                   8/2/   ON CIVIL RIGHTS.
-ENG/SOT-   -ENG/SOT-

Page 5 (Script sheet) This is the first appearance of an over-the-shoulder 1-shot of Denise. This is also the first appearance of a violator, which is on still-store 8, keyed over videotape #21 (VT 21).

REPORTER/WRITER Kocly   PAGE 5

CHYRON/ENG SHEET

| | 6:30AM | NOON | 6:00PM | 11:00PM | OTHER |

DATE: 4-29-92

EDITOR: 9   Baltimore Revels

TIME	AUDIO	SUPER TIME IN	OUT	CHYRON INFORMATION	CHYRON ADDRESS
00	SOT			Emmett	(571)
		00	20	~~Emmett~~ Burns NAACP	
				~~Street sign~~	(572)
		27	36	Officer Innes Foster	
		37	43	Officer Milton Krysztofiak	(573)
		50	100	Javier Avila Californian	(574)
		135	146	Billy Murphy attorney	(575)
146	out			Arafa?	

BLACK TIME: 148

WJZ-TV 13

Page 5 (Chyron/ENG sheet) This contains the list of addresses the director must call up to better identify the subjects in the videotape package.

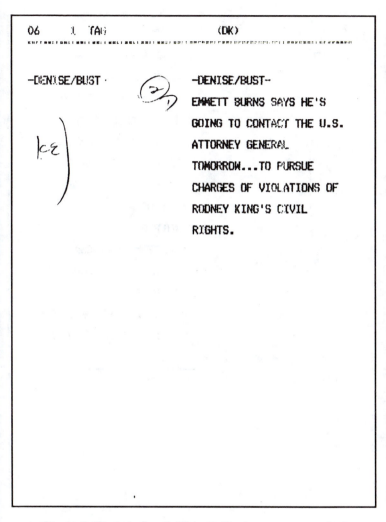

06   1   TAG   (DK)

-DENISE/BUST   -DENISE/BUST-

                                       EMMETT BURNS SAYS HE'S

                                       GOING TO CONTACT THE U.S.

      ck   ATTORNEY GENERAL

                                       TOMORROW...TO PURSUE

                                       CHARGES OF VIOLATIONS OF

                                       RODNEY KING'S CIVIL

                                       RIGHTS.

Page 6 (Script sheet) This indicates a camera 1 chromakey (1ck); camera 2 remains Denise's primary camera.

```
07      1   PIGTOWN FOLO        AS (AS)
```

```
AL BUST                       --- AL BUST ---

                              TONIGHT IN BALTIMORE,

                              POLICE ARE FIGHTING TO

                              HELP THE CHILDREN THEY

                              TOOK AN OATH TO PROTECT.

                              THEY'RE DOING EVERYTHING

                              THEY CAN TO KEEP THE

                              DOORS OF A RECREATION

                              CENTER OPEN. THE

                              NIGHTTEAM'S MELISSA

                              SANDER SHOWS US HOW THE

                              CLUB GETS CHILDREN OFF
                                      22
                              THE STREETS AND AWAY FROM

                              THE CRIME THAT COULD KILL

                              THEM.

ENG SOT                       --- ENG SOT ---
```

REPORTER/WRITER __MELISSA / CORKRAN__   PAGE __7__

CHYRON/ENG SHEET

DATE: __4-29-92__   6:30AM   NOON   6:00PM   (11:00PM)   OTHER

EDITOR: __HARRIET__   PIGTOWN FOLO

TIME	AUDIO	SUPER TIME IN	OUT	CHYRON INFORMATION	CHYRON ADDRESS
00	SOT	00	05	BAYARD ST.	(576)
		11	(16)	DONTA BRAXTON / 17 YEARS OLD	(577)
		17	23	RHONDA McCAIN / 14 YEARS OLD	(578)
		36	41	MELISSA SANDER (#8)	(579)
		43	52	OFFICER CHARLES BENJAMIN / BALTIMORE POLICE	(520)
		108	(112)	CHARLES PEACOCK / 15 YEARS OLD	(521)
				~~COUNCILMAN JOE DISTRICT~~	~~522~~
		130	136	VOICE OF:	(522)
150	OUT			Eyewitness news."	
				BLACK TIME: 153	

WJZ-TV 13

```
08     1   TAG                    (AS)
```

AL. BUST   ---- AL BUST ----

THE BALTIMORE POLICE
YOUTH CENTERS BEGAN IN
1947...THERE WERE FOUR OF
THEM...THE OTHER THREE
CLOSED IN THE 1970'S AND
80'S.

OY   I   WAKE-UP WEATHER   (UK)

DENISE BUST   --- DENISE BUST ---

A LITTLE BIT OF SUN.... A
LITTLE BIT OF CLOUDS....
SOMETHING FOR EVERYONE IN
BOB'S WAKIN UP FORECAST.

Page 9 (Script sheet) The word *forecast* has been circled by the newscast director by force of habit; it has no special significance.

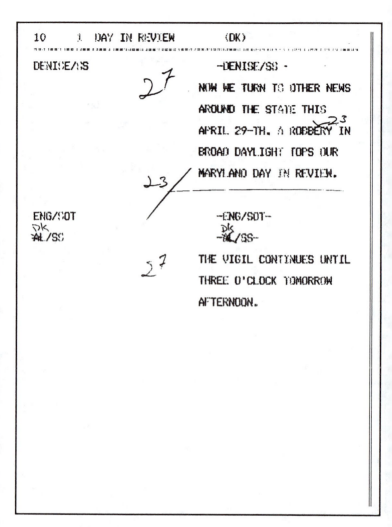

```
10      1 DAY IN REVIEW          (DK)

DENISE/SS                    -DENISE/SS -

                             NOW WE TURN TO OTHER NEWS

                             AROUND THE STATE THIS

                             APRIL 29-TH. A ROBBERY IN

                             BROAD DAYLIGHT TOPS OUR

                             MARYLAND DAY IN REVIEW.



ENG/SOT                      -ENG/SOT-
DK                              DK
AL/SS                        -AL/SS-

                             THE VIGIL CONTINUES UNTIL

                             THREE O'CLOCK TOMORROW

                             AFTERNOON.
```

Page 10 (Script sheet) This is the first appearance of an over-the-shoulder still-store graphic for the "Day in Review" segment of the program. There is also a note for playback of videotape machine #23 and ENG sound-on-tape.

REPORTER/WRITER_____   PAGE __/0__

CHYRON/ENG SHEET

DATE: __4·29__   6:30AM   NOON   6:00PM   (11:00PM)   OTHER

EDITOR: __Roz__   Day In Review

TIME	AUDIO	SUPER TIME IN	OUT	CHYRON INFORMATION	CHYRON ADDRESS
00	SOT				
101	out			"... of rembrance"	
				BLACK TIME: 1:04	

WJZ-TV 13

Page 10 (Chyron/ENG sheet) This is notable because it contains the phrase ". . . of remembrance." This is the outcue for the 1:01 minute "Day in Review" package; it tells the director when to tell the technical director to switch to the camera 3 bust on the following script.

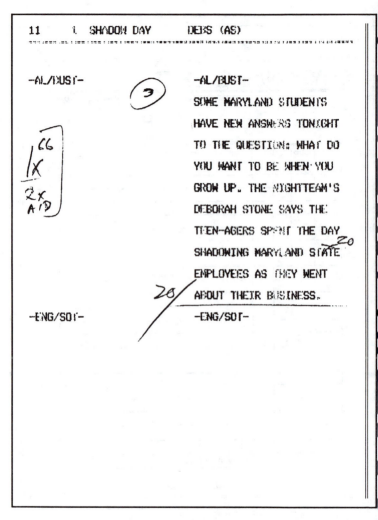

```
11      1. SHADOW DAY      DEBS (AS)

-AL/BUST-                    -AL/BUST-
                    (3)      SOME MARYLAND STUDENTS
                            HAVE NEW ANSWERS TONIGHT
   CG                       TO THE QUESTION: WHAT DO
   X                        YOU WANT TO BE WHEN YOU
   2X                       GROW UP. THE NIGHTTEAM'S
   A/D                      DEBORAH STONE SAYS THE
                            TEEN-AGERS SPENT THE DAY
                                                    20
                            SHADOWING MARYLAND STATE
                            EMPLOYEES AS THEY WENT
                        20/ ABOUT THEIR BUSINESS.
-ENG/SOT-                    -ENG/SOT-
```

Page 11 (Script sheet) This is the first appearance of a 2-shot (of Al and Denise) on camera 1, with camera 6 in effects.

REPORTER/WRITER ___BOB STONE___   PAGE ___11___

CHYRON/ENG SHEET

| | 6:30AM | NOON | 6:00PM | (11:00PM) | OTHER |

DATE: ___3-29-97___

EDITOR: _____   SNOW DAY

E⁻ 1893

TIME	AUDIO	SUPER TIME IN	OUT	CHYRON INFORMATION	CHYRON ADDRESS
00	00				
		00		TAPE IS	500
		07	15		
		32	37	JANE WEATHERLY	501
				S-TV REPORTER/ANCHOR	
		55	02	THOMAS SCOTT	502
				10C YOR CORPS	
		03	08	TONY STEVENSON	503
				AUTO BODY REPAIR SPECIALIST	
		04	11	JOE KING FM	504
		25	31	JUAN SNYDER	505
				10TH GRADER	
51	00			E N.	

BLACK TIME: 1:53

WJZ-TV 13

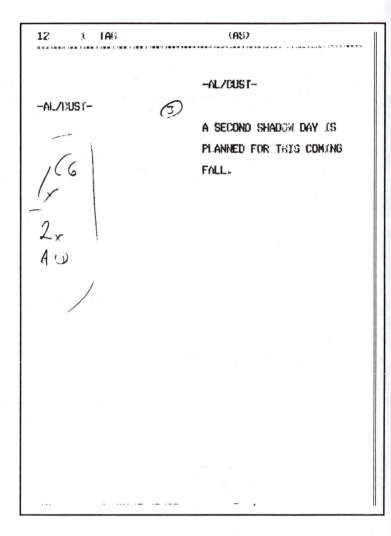

Page 12 (Script sheet) This features a bust on camera 3, turning to camera 1 on a 2-shot F/X with camera 6 in the window for the sports tease.

```
13    1  S-TEASE SPORTS        (D/A)
```

DENISE/2SHOT/EFFEX	−DENISE/2SHOT/EFFEX−
	LOTS MORE AHEAD ON
	EYEWITNESS NEWS...
AL/2SHOT/EFFEX	−AL/2SHOT/EFFEX−
	INCLUDING SPORTS WITH
	JOHN BUREN...
NEW1	WHO'S IN THE PALACE, OF
	COURSE, WITH A PREVIEW.
	BEVO???
JOHN	−JOHN−
	BLAH. BLAH.
AL/2SHOT	−AL/2SHOT−
	THANKS, JOHN. BOB'S NEXT
	WITH THE FORECAST.
DENISE/COLD/ENG/VO	−DENISE/COLD/ENG/VO−
	LATER ON... A DEADLY

Page 13 (Script sheet) This notes a camera 6 ZOOM; there is also a setup on camera 2 for a 2-shot front and center (of Al and Denise).

```
13      2  S-TEASE SPORTS
                          COLLISION AT A RAILROAD
                          CROSSING SPARKS AN AMTRAK
                          DERAILMENT.

AL/WIPE/ENG/VO        CC/LL  -AL/WIPE/ENG/VO-
                          AND A VACATION-TURNED
                          NIGHTMARE.... DETAILS IN
                          OUR WORLD WRAP.
```

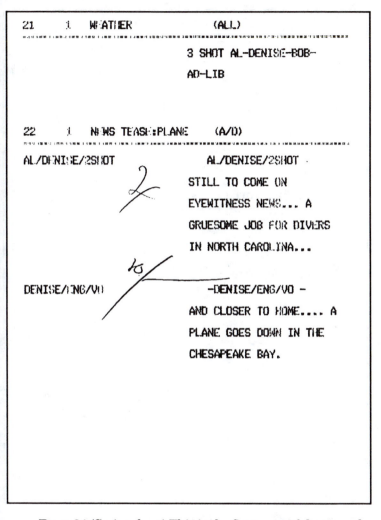

```
21     1    WEATHER              (ALL)
==================================================================
                             3 SHOT AL-DENISE-BOB-
                             AD-LIB



22     1    NEWS TEASE:PLANE    (A/D)
==================================================================
AL/DENISE/2SHOT              AL/DENISE/2SHOT
                             STILL TO COME ON
                             EYEWITNESS NEWS... A
                             GRUESOME JOB FOR DIVERS
                             IN NORTH CAROLINA...

DENISE/ENG/VO               -DENISE/ENG/VO -
                             AND CLOSER TO HOME.... A
                             PLANE GOES DOWN IN THE
                             CHESAPEAKE BAY.
```

Page 21 (Script sheet) This is the first page of the second segment of the show. It is blank because the weather is always ad-libbed—performed with a wireless microphone system without a script. The total running time of this section is carefully monitored by the producer so that she can compensate for a show that may be running "heavy" or "light."

```
*****  1   **SPOTS 2***********  (****)


             1   $$$$ LOTTERY $$$$
```

Spots This page is blank because the commercial spots are inserted by the computerized Betacart system.

Lottery The daily numbers are called up from the still-store and inserted with the spots.

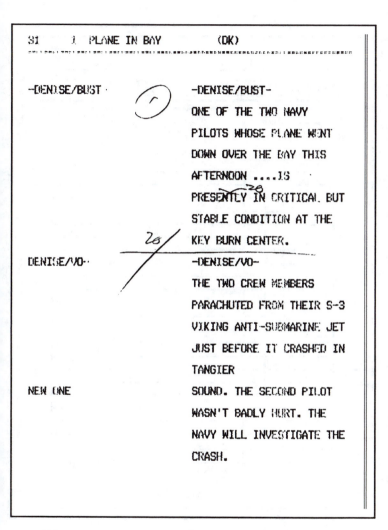

31   1 PLANE IN BAY   (DK)

-DENISE/BUST-

-DENISE/BUST-

ONE OF THE TWO NAVY
PILOTS WHOSE PLANE WENT
DOWN OVER THE BAY THIS
AFTERNOON ....IS
PRESENTLY IN CRITICAL BUT
STABLE CONDITION AT THE
KEY BURN CENTER.

DENISE/VO-

-DENISE/VO-

THE TWO CREW MEMBERS
PARACHUTED FROM THEIR S-3
VIKING ANTI-SUBMARINE JET
JUST BEFORE IT CRASHED IN
TANGIER

NEW ONE

SOUND. THE SECOND PILOT
WASN'T BADLY HURT. THE
NAVY WILL INVESTIGATE THE
CRASH.

Page 31 (Script sheet) This brings the newscast back
from the spots to camera 1 with a bust shot of Denise.

REPORTER/WRITER *Crow*   PAGE *31*

CHYRON/ENG SHEET

DATE: *4/29/92*   6:30AM   NOON   6:00PM   (11:00PM)   OTHER

EDITOR: *MC*   *Plane In Bay*

TIME	AUDIO	SUPER TIME IN	OUT	CHYRON INFORMATION	CHYRON ADDRESS
00	NAT				
				CTSY WMDT	506
30	out				
			BLACK TIME:		

WJZ-TV 13

Page 31 (Chyron/ENG sheet) This is the first appearance of voiceover (VO) with a total running time of audio at 30 seconds. This material is courtesy of WMDT, Chyron address 506; there is no time indicated, which means it can be inserted anywhere over the video.

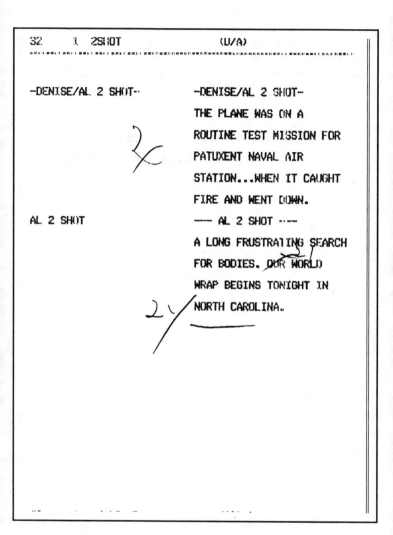

```
32    1  2SHOT                    (U/A)
-----------------------------------------------

-DENISE/AL 2 SHOT-           -DENISE/AL 2 SHOT-

                             THE PLANE WAS ON A

                             ROUTINE TEST MISSION FOR

                             PATUXENT NAVAL AIR

                             STATION...WHEN IT CAUGHT

                             FIRE AND WENT DOWN.

AL 2 SHOT                    ---- AL 2 SHOT ----

                             A LONG FRUSTRATING SEARCH

                             FOR BODIES. OUR WORLD

                             WRAP BEGINS TONIGHT IN

                             NORTH CAROLINA.
```

Page 32 (Script sheet) Standard 2-shot on camera 2, with a turn camera 3 still-store 7 over-the-shoulder to "World Wrap" graphic.

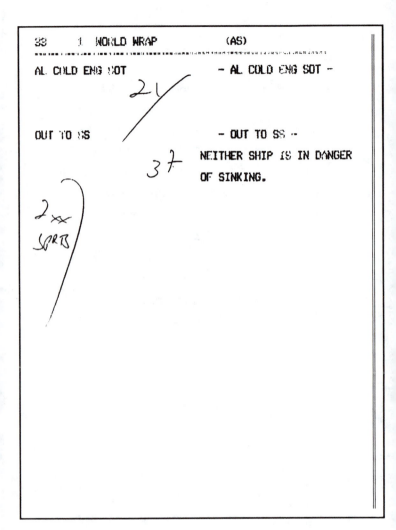

33   1   WORLD WRAP   (AS)

AL. COLD ENG SOT   - AL. COLD ENG SOT -

OUT TO SS   - OUT TO SS -

                                   NEITHER SHIP IS IN DANGER
                                   OF SINKING.

Page 33 (Script sheet) Continue and end of "World Wrap."

REPORTER/WRITER_____   PAGE___*33*___

CHYRON/ENG SHEET

| | 6:30AM | NOON | 6:00PM | (11:00PM) | OTHER |

DATE:_____

EDITOR:_____

TIME	AUDIO	SUPER TIME IN	OUT	CHYRON INFORMATION	CHYRON ADDRESS
				is un known	

BLACK TIME: 42

WJZ-TV 13

Page 33 (Chyron/ENG) This is the playback of ENG/SOT. Running time is 38 seconds; outcue unknown.

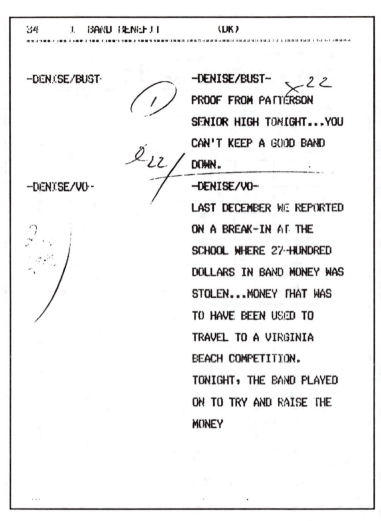

Page 34 (Script sheet) This material was killed to make up for 33 second heavy running time that is indicated at the beginning of the column marked BKTIME in the rundown.

REPORTER/WRITER _____   PAGE **34**

CHYRON/ENG SHEET

DATE: **4/29/92**   6:30AM   NOON   6:00PM   11:00PM   OTHER

EDITOR: _____

Band Benefit

TIME	AUDIO	SUPER TIME IN	OUT	CHYRON INFORMATION	CHYRON ADDRESS
00	MS				
		on	is	Patterson HS	(507)
30	out				
			BLACK TIME:		

WJZ-TV 13

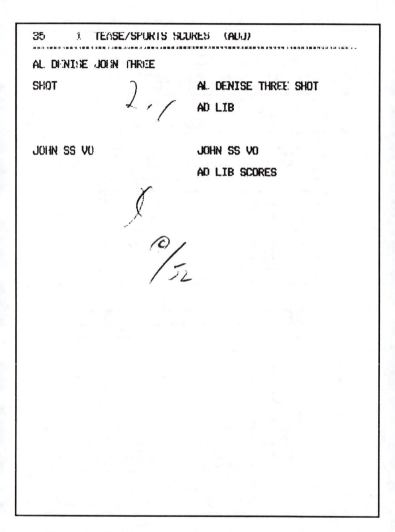

Page 35 (Script sheet) This is the first appearance of a 3-shot (sports tease), coming off an over-the-shoulder of Al to camera 2. This is also a note to dissolve to the Chyron over VT #52.

REPORTER/WRITER _____   PAGE___t-e 2____

CHYRON/ENG SHEET

DATE:__4-29__   6:30AM   NOON   6:00PM   11:00PM   OTHER

EDITOR:_____   sports scores

CHYRON INFORMATION	CHYRON ADDRESS
National	
chicago	
atlanta	
st louis	
san francisco	
pittsburgh	
cinncinnati	
houston	
ny mets	
NHL	
ny rangers	
new jersey	
montreal	
hartford	
boston	
buffalo	

WJZ-TV 13

Sports scores (Chyron/ENG sheet) Note for National League and NHL.

Sports scores (Chyron/ENG sheet) Note for American League.

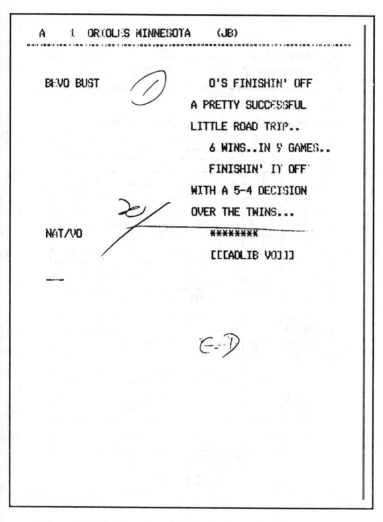

    A   1   ORIOLES MINNESOTA   (JB)

    BEVO BUST   O'S FINISHIN' OFF

                                        A PRETTY SUCCESSFUL

                                        LITTLE ROAD TRIP..

                                            6 WINS..IN 9 GAMES..

                                        FINISHIN' IT OFF

                                        WITH A 5-4 DECISION

                                        OVER THE TWINS...

    NAT/VO   ********

                                        [[[ADLIB VO]]]

Page A (Script sheet) This is a 3-shot on camera 2, turning to camera 1 with a bust shot.

REPORTER/WRITER _____   PAGE ___a___

CHYRON/ENG SHEET

	6:30AM	NOON	6:00PM	11:00PM	OTHER

DATE: ___2* 4-29___

EDITOR: ___Mickey___   o*ioles minnesota

TIME	AUDIO	SUPER TIME IN	OUT	CHYRON INFORMATION	CHYRON ADDRESS
00	VO)				
		00	05	minneapolis	
				courtesy twinsvision	
		35	40	orioles 5	
				minnesota 4	
48					

BLACK TIME: __50__

WJZ-TV 13

Page A (Chyron/ENG sheet) This is a voiceover (VO) Orioles-Minnesota game score.

Page B This page was killed by producer and does not appear in the script.

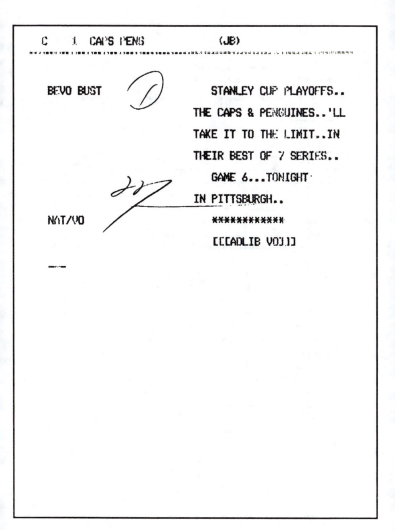

C   1   CAPS PENS   (JB)

BEVO BUST   STANLEY CUP PLAYOFFS..
                   THE CAPS & PENGUINES..'LL
                   TAKE IT TO THE LIMIT..IN
                   THEIR BEST OF 7 SERIES..
                   GAME 6...TONIGHT·
                   IN PITTSBURGH..
NAT/VO   ************
                   [[[ADLIB VO]]]

Page C (Script sheet) Bust shot with playback of Stanley Cup playoffs on VT #22.

REPORTER/WRITER_____   PAGE____C____

CHYRON/ENG SHEET

6:30AM   NOON   6:00PM   11:00PM   OTHER

DATE:____4-29____

EDITOR:____Misky____   cape pens

TIME	AUDIO	SUPER TIME IN	OUT	CHYRON INFORMATION	CHYRON ADDRESS
00	No				
		00	05	pittsburgh	
				courtesy khl sports	
		15	20	washington	
				pittsburgh	
31	out				

BLACK TIME: 83

WJZ-TV 13

Page C (Chyron/ENG sheet) Capitols-Penguins score.

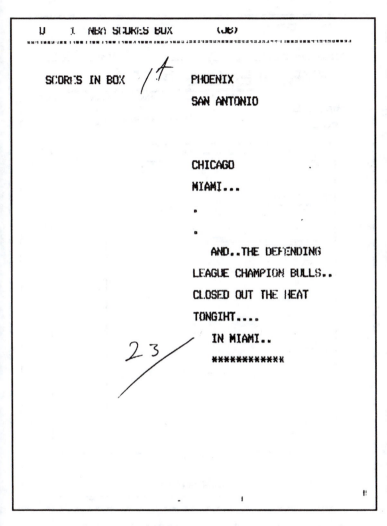

Page D (Script sheet) Camera 1 ADO with over-the-shoulder for John with NBA scores. Newscast director notes a roll cue on VT #23 to begin with words "in Miami. . . ."

REPORTER/WRITER_____   PAGE___D___

CHYRON/ENG SHEET

| | 6:30AM | NOON | 6:00PM | 11:00PM | OTHER |

DATE:___4-29___

EDITOR:_____

nba score in box

CHYRON INFORMATION	CHYRON ADDRESS
nba	
phoenix	
san antonio	
chicago	
miami	

WJZ-TV 13

Page D (Chyron/ENG sheet) NBA scores.

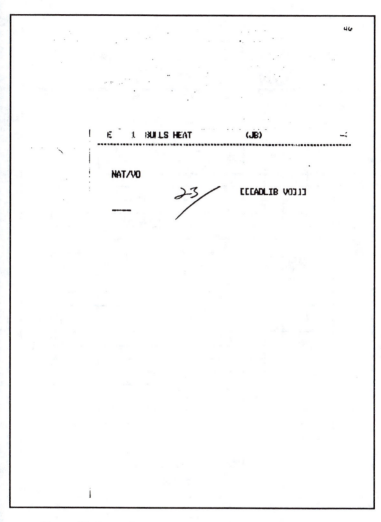

Page E (Script sheet) VT #23 footage with John ad-libbing his VO.

REPORTER/WRITER_____   PAGE_____ 0

CHYRON/ENG SHEET

| | 6:30AM | NOON | 6:00PM | 11:00PM | OTHER |

DATE: 4-29

EDITOR: Micky

bull- heat

TIME	AUDIO	SUPER TIME IN	OUT	CHYRON INFORMATION	CHYRON ADDRESS
00	not				
				no ciy nee-e-	
27	on				
			BLACK TIME: 29		

WJZ-TV 13

Page E (Chyron/ENG sheet) Bulls-Heat score.

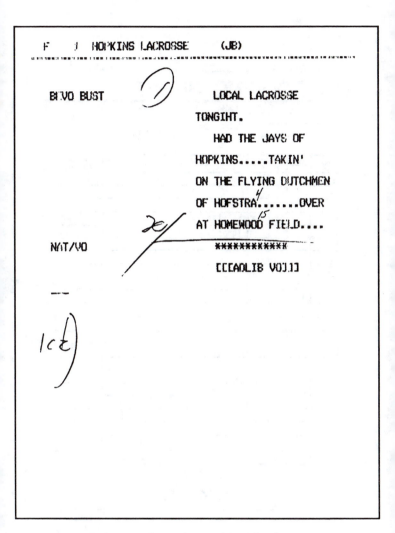

Page F (Script sheet) Bust shot of John on camera 1, leading to playback on VT #20.

REPORTER/WRITER_____ PAGE____ f

CHYRON/ENG SHEET

| | 8:30AM | NOON | 6:00PM | 11:00PM | OTHER |

DATE:____4-29____

EDITOR:____Micky____   hopkins lacrosse

TIME	AUDIO	SUPER TIME IN	OUT	CHYRON INFORMATION	CHYRON ADDRESS
∞	NOT				
		18	23	hofstra	
				johns hopkins	
31	SAT				
			BLACK TIME: 33	

WJZ-TV 13

Page F (Chyron/ENG sheet) Hopkins lacrosse score.

```
42    1   AROUND TOWN              (B1)
━━━━━━━━━━━━━━━━━━━━━━━━━━━━━━━━━━━━━━━━━━━━━━━━━━━━━━━━━━━━━━━━━━━━━


                         /c ?



44    1   BYE/CREDITS-DR 27:15 (ALL)
━━━━━━━━━━━━━━━━━━━━━━━━━━━━━━━━━━━━━━━━━━━━━━━━━━━━━━━━━━━━━━━━━━━━━

DK THREE SHOT          DK THREE SHOT
                       THAT'S OUR REPORT. A
                       SPECIAL EDITION OF
***NEW 1               NIGHTLINE IS NEXT... ON
                       THE VERDICT IN THE POLICE
                       BEATING TRIAL OF MOTORIST
                       RODNEY KING. I'M DENISE
                       KOCH.
   AL THREE SHOT          AL THREE SHOT
                       AND I'M AL SANDERS. FOR
                       THE ENTIRE EYEWITNESS
                       NEWS TEAM...GOOD NIGHT.
```

Page 42 (Script sheet) This is camera 1 in chromakey for "Around Town."

Page 43 (Script sheet) This page was killed by the producer.

Page 44 (Script sheet) Turning to a 3-shot (all) for the bye credits.

APPENDIX 3

Designated Market Areas
Ranked by Size (January 1993)

Rank	DMA	No. of TV Households	% of U.S. Households
1.	New York	6,733,920	7.237
2.	Los Angeles	4,965,760	5.336
3.	Chicago	3,028,500	3.255
4.	Philadelphia	2,658,130	2.857
5.	San Francisco–Oakland–San Jose	2,246,220	2.414
6.	Boston	2,109,390	2.267
7.	Washington, D.C.	1,851,480	1.990
8.	Dallas–Ft. Worth	1,803,680	1.938
9.	Detroit	1,723,460	1.852
10.	Atlanta	1,475,590	1.586
11.	Houston	1,455,000	1.564
12.	Cleveland	1,442,370	1.550
13.	Seattle–Tacoma	1,389,810	1.494
14.	Tampa–St. Petersburg–Sarasota	1,374,310	1.477
15.	Minneapolis–St. Paul	1,369,670	1.472
16.	Miami–Ft. Lauderdale	1,291,940	1.388
17.	Pittsburgh	1,126,760	1.211
18.	St. Louis	1,102,600	1.185
19.	Sacramento–Stockton–Modesto	1,082,200	1.163
20.	Phoenix	1,068,050	1.148
21.	Denver	1,034,000	1.111
22.	Baltimore	966,110	1.038

*Reprinted by permission of A. C. Nielsen Media Research, Inc.

Rank	DMA	No. of TV Households	% of U.S. Households
23.	Orlando–Daytona–Melbourne	947,330	1.018
24.	Hartford–New Haven	930,870	1.000
25.	San Diego	910,990	0.979
26.	Indianapolis	895,790	0.963
27.	Portland, OR	867,780	0.933
28.	Milwaukee	771,520	0.829
29.	Kansas City	760,020	0.817
30.	Charlotte	758,710	0.815
31.	Cincinnati	756,230	0.813
32.	Raleigh–Durham	728,290	0.783
33.	Nashville	727,150	0.781
34.	Columbus, OH	678,420	0.729
35.	Greenville–Spartanburg–Asheville	656,130	0.705
36.	Grand Rapids–Kalamazoo–Battle Creek	634,720	0.682
37.	Buffalo	628,760	0.676
38.	Norfolk–Portsmouth–Newport News	614,640	0.661
39.	San Antonio	605,200	0.650
40.	New Orleans	600,770	0.646
41.	Salt Lake City	600,230	0.645
42.	Memphis	590,100	0.634
43.	Providence–New Bedford	567,110	0.609
44.	Harrisburg–Lancaster–Lebanon–York	564,990	0.607
45.	Oklahoma City	562,920	0.605
46.	West Palm Beach–Ft. Pierce	559,670	0.601
47.	Wilkes Barre–Scranton	546,050	0.587
48.	Greensboro–High Point–Winston Salem	530,140	0.570
49.	Albuquerque–Santa Fe	521,930	0.561
50.	Louisville	519,830	0.559
51.	Birmingham	514,640	0.553
52.	Albany–Schenectady–Troy	507,360	0.545
53.	Dayton	503,440	0.541
54.	Richmond–Petersburg	476,850	0.512
55.	Jacksonville–Brunswick	473,030	0.508
56.	Charleston–Huntington	465,250	0.500
57.	Fresno–Visalia	463,760	0.498
58.	Little Rock–Pine Bluff	455,320	0.489
59.	Tulsa	444,690	0.478

Rank	DMA	No. of TV Households	% of U.S. Households
60.	Flint–Saginaw–Bay City	444,100	0.477
61.	Wichita–Hutchinson	416,280	0.447
62.	Mobile–Pensacola	412,770	0.444
63.	Knoxville	406,670	0.437
64.	Toledo	405,800	0.436
65.	Roanoke–Lynchburg	382,710	0.411
66.	Syracuse	380,010	0.408
67.	Austin	373,670	0.402
68.	Green Bay–Appleton	371,470	0.399
69.	Shreveport	368,700	0.396
70.	Honolulu	363,360	0.390
71.	Lexington	359,890	0.387
72.	Rochester, NY	359,570	0.386
73.	Des Moines–Ames	354,710	0.381
74.	Portland–Auburn	346,020	0.372
75.	Omaha	344,780	0.371
76.	Paducah–Cape Giradeau–Harrisburg–Mt Vernon	343,260	0.369
77.	Champaign–Springfield–Decatur	340,050	0.365
78.	Las Vegas	333,050	0.358
79.	Spokane	324,870	0.349
80.	Springfield MO	320,400	0.344
81.	Tucson (Nogales)	314,490	0.338
82.	Chattanooga	310,190	0.333
83.	South Bend–Elkhart	298,320	0.321
84.	Cedar Rapids–Waterloo–Dubuque	295,480	0.318
85.	Madison	293,280	0.315
86.	Ft. Myers–Naples	293,110	0.315
87.	Burlington–Plattsburgh	292,900	0.315
88.	Davenport–Rock Island–Moline	291,550	0.313
89.	Columbia SC	290,740	0.312
90.	Huntsville–Decatur FL	289,510	0.311
91.	Jackson, MS	284,970	0.306
92.	Tri–Cities TN–VA	280,770	0.302
93.	Johnstown–Altoona	276,230	0.297
94.	Youngstown	269,760	0.290
95.	Evansville	266,410	0.286
96.	Baton Rougue	252,840	0.272
97.	Waco–Temple–Bryan	251,530	0.270

Rank	DMA	No. of TV Households	% of U.S. Households
98.	Lincoln–Hastings–Kearney (Plus)	250,360	0.269
99.	Springfield–Holyoke	247,520	0.266
100.	Colorado Springs–Pueblo	241,950	0.260
101.	El Paso	238,710	0.257
102.	Ft. Wayne	236,020	0.254
103.	Savannah	234,490	0.252
104.	Lansing	228,330	0.245
105.	Greenville–New Bern–Washington	227,340	0.244
106.	Charleston, SC	225,180	0.242
107.	Sioux Falls (Mitchell)	219,910	0.236
108.	Fargo–Valley City	213,670	0.230
109.	Santa Barbara–Santa Maria–San Luis Obispo	210,820	0.227
110.	Montgomery	207,310	0.223
111.	Monterey–Salinas	206,370	0.222
112.	Peoria–Bloomington	204,970	0.220
113.	Augusta	202,780	0.218
114.	Harlingen–Weslaco–Brownsville	198,450	0.213
115.	Eugene	195,100	0.210
116.	Tallahassee–Thomasville	194,750	0.209
117.	Reno	190,860	0.205
118.	Lafayette, LA	190,730	0.205
119.	Ft. Smith	190,390	0.205
120.	Macon	182,490	0.196
121.	Tyler	182,160	0.196
122.	Traverse City–Cadillac	180,770	0.194
123.	Columbus, GA	180,000	0.193
124.	Yakima–Pasco–Richland–Kennewick	172,410	0.185
125.	Chico–Redding	168,490	0.181
126.	Bakersfield	167,660	0.180
127.	Duluth–Superior	167,430	0.180
128.	Amarillo	167,170	0.180
129.	Monroe–El Dorado	166,810	0.179
130.	Florence–Myrtle Beach	165,920	0.178
131.	Corpus Christi	165,630	0.178
132.	Wausau–Rhinelander	163,170	0.175
133.	Columbus–Tupelo–West Point MS	163,050	0.175
134.	La Crosse–Eau Claire	161,880	0.174
135.	Boise	158,310	0.170

Rank	DMA	No. of TV Households	% of U.S. Households
136.	Wheeling–Steubenville	156,610	0.168
137.	Beaumont–Port Arthur	156,520	0.168
138.	Rockford	156,210	0.168
139.	Topeka	152,950	0.164
140.	Wichita Falls–Lawton	150,560	0.162
141.	Erie	149,070	0.160
142.	Sioux City	148,920	0.160
143.	Terra Haute	148,630	0.160
144.	Wilmington	148,000	0.159
145.	Rochester MN–Mason City IA–Austin MN	139,790	0.150
146.	Medford–Klamath Falls	139,760	0.150
147.	Joplin MO–Pittsburgh KS	136,990	0.147
148.	Binghamton	136,020	0.146
149.	Lubbock	133,590	0.144
150.	Columbia–Jefferson City	132,320	0.142
151.	Bluefield–Beckley– Oak Hill	132,210	0.142
152.	Odessa–Midland	129,990	0.140
153.	Minot–Bismarck–Dickinson	129,310	0.139
154.	Albany GA	127,520	0.137
155.	Bangor	124,750	0.134
156.	Palm Springs	115,280	0.124
157.	Anchorage	112,210	0.121
158.	Quincy IL–Hannibal–MO–Keokuk IA	109,470	0.118
159.	Abilene–Sweetwater	106,800	0.115
160.	Biloxi–Gulfport	102,590	0.110
161.	Clarksburg–Weston	100,370	0.108
162.	Idaho Falls–Pocatello	100,210	0.108
163.	Utica	97,890	0.105
164.	Dothan	97,330	0.105
165.	Salisbury	96,430	0.104
166.	Elmira	93,300	0.100
167.	Gainesville	89,810	0.097
168.	Hattiesburg–Laurel	89,130	.096
169.	Panama City	87,980	.095
170.	Alexandria LA	84,210	.090
171.	Billings	82,950	.089
172.	Rapid City	82,780	.089
173.	Greenwood–Greenville	76,720	.082

Rank	DMA	No. of TV Households	% of U.S. Households
174.	Watertown	75,480	.081
175.	Jonesboro	74,230	.080
176.	Lake Charles	73,700	.079
177.	Missoula	73,110	.079
178.	Yuma–El Centro	70,280	.076
179.	Ada–Ardmore	70,110	.075
180.	Marquette	69,890	.075
181.	Meridian	63,890	.069
182.	Great Falls	62,020	.067
183.	Parkersburg	59,890	.064
184.	St. Joseph	57,850	.062
185.	Jackson, TN	57,260	.062
186.	Mankato	56,780	.061
187.	Tuscaloosa	56,060	.060
188.	Eureka	55,210	.059
189.	Grand Junction–Montrose	55,100	.059
190.	Bowling Green	50,710	.054
191.	Butte	48,140	.052
192.	San Angelo	47,180	.051
193.	Lafayette, IN	45,770	.049
194.	Casper–Riverton	45,480	.049
195.	Charlottesville	43,560	.047
196.	Anniston	42,820	.046
197	Cheyenne–Scottsbluff–Sterling	42,370	.046
198.	Ottumwa–Kirksville	41,220	.044
199.	Lima	39,210	.042
200.	Laredo	38,770	.042
201.	Harrisonburg	37,560	.040
202.	Zanesville	30,790	.033
203.	Twin Falls	30,660	.033
204.	Presque Isle	30,640	.033
205.	Bend OR	30,560	.033
206.	Fairbanks	29,880	.032
207.	Victoria	25,770	.028
208.	Helena	18,790	.020
209.	Alpena	15,870	.017
210.	North Platte	14,180	.015
211.	Glendive	4,300	.005

APPENDIX 4

Nationwide Compendium of Local Television News Stations

(by DMA size)

1. New York, NY

WABC–TV
7 Lincoln Sq.
New York, NY 10023
212–456–7777

WCBS–TV
524 W. 57th St.
New York, NY 10019
212–975–4321

WNBC–TV
30 Rockefeller Plaza
New York, NY 10020
212–664–4444

WNYC–TV (noncommercial)
One Centre St.
New York, NY 10007
212–669–7800

WNYW
205 E. 67th St.
New York, NY 10021
212–452–5555

WPIX
11 WPIX Plaza
New York, NY 10017
212–949–1100

WWOR–TV
9 Broadcast Plaza
Secaucus, NJ 07096
201–348–0009

2. Los Angeles, CA

KCET (noncommercial)
4401 Sunset Blvd.
Hollywood, CA 90027
213–666–6500

KABC–TV
4151 Prospect Ave.
Los Angeles, CA 90027
310–557–7777

KCAL
5515 Melrose Ave.
Los Angeles, CA 90038
213–467–9999

KCBS–TV
6121 Sunset Blvd.
Los Angeles, CA 90028
213–460–3000

KCOP
915 N. La Brea Ave.
Los Angeles, CA 90038
213–851–1000

KMEX–TV (Univision)
6255 Sunset Blvd., 16th Fl.
Hollywood, CA 90028
213–960–3313

KNBC–TV
3000 W. Alameda Ave.
Burbank, CA 91523
818–840–4444

KTLA
5800 Sunset Blvd.
Los Angeles, CA 90078
213–460–5500

KVEA
1130A Air Way
Glendale, CA 91201
818–502–5700

KWHY–TV
5545 Sunset Blvd.
Los Angeles, CA 90028
213–466–5441

KTTV (Fox)
5746 Sunset Blvd.
Los Angeles, CA 90028
213–856–1000

3. Chicago, IL

WBBM–TV (CBS)
630 N. McClurg Ct.
Chicago, IL 60611
312–944–6000

WCIU–TV
141 W. Jackson Blvd.
Chicago, IL 60604
312–663–0260

WFLD (Fox)
205 N. Michigan Ave.
Chicago, IL 60601
312–565–5532

WGN–TV
2501 Bradley Pl.
Chicago, IL 60618
312–528–2311

WLS–TV (ABC)
190 N. State St.
Chicago, IL 60601
312–750–7777

WMAQ–TV (NBC)
454 N. Columbus Dr.
Chicago, IL 60611
312–836–5555

WSNS (Telemundo)
430 W. Grant Pl.
Chicago, IL 60614
312–929–1200

4. Philadelphia, PA

KYW–TV (NBC)
Independence Mall East
Philadelphia, PA 19106
215–238–4700

WCAU–TV (CBS)
City Ave. & Monument Rd.
Philadelphia, PA 19131
215–668–5510

WPVI–TV (ABC)
4100 City Line Ave.
Philadelphia, PA 19131
215–878–9700

WTXF–TV (Fox)
330 Market St.
Philadelphia, PA 19106
215–925–2929

5. San Francisco–Oakland–San Jose, CA

KDTV (Univision)
2200 Palou Ave.
San Francisco, CA 94124
415–641–1400

KGO–TV (ABC)
900 Front St.
San Francisco, CA 94111
415–954–7777

KPIX (CBS)
855 Battery St.
San Francisco, CA 94111
415–362–5550

KRON–TV (NBC)
1001 Van Ness Ave.
San Francisco, CA 94109
415–441–4444

KTSF
100 Valley Dr.
Brisbane, CA 94005
415–468–2626

KTVU (Fox)
Box 22222
Oakland, CA 94623
510–834–1212

KICU–TV
1585 Schallenberger Rd.
San Jose, CA 95131
408–298–3636

KNTV (ABC)
645 Park Ave.
San Jose, CA 95110
408–286–1111

KSTS (Telemundo)
2349 Bering Dr.
San Jose, CA 95131
408–435–8848

6. Boston, MA

WBZ–TV (NBC)
1170 Soldiers Field Rd.
Boston, MA 02134
617–787–7000

WCVB–TV (ABC)
5 TV Pl.
Needham, MA 02194
617–449–0400

WGBH–TV (noncommercial)
125 Western Ave.
Boston, MA 02134
617–492–2777

WHDH–TV (CBS)
7 Bulfinch Pl.
Boston, MA 02114
617–725–0777

WLVI–TV
75 Morrissey Blvd.
Boston, MA 02125
617–265–5656

7. Washington, DC

WETA–TV (noncommercial)
Box 2626
Washington, DC 20013
703–998–2600

WJLA–TV (ABC)
3007 Tilden St., NW
Washington, DC 20008
202–364–7777

WRC–TV (NBC)
4001 Nebraska Ave., NW
Washington, DC 20016
202–885–4000

WTTG (Fox)
5151 Wisconsin Ave., NW
Washington, DC 20016
202–244–5151

WUSA (CBS)
4100 Wisconsin Ave., NW
Washington, DC 20016
202–895–5999

8. Dallas–Fort Worth, TX

KDFW–TV (CBS)
400 N. Griffin
Dallas, TX 75202
214–720–4444

KXTX–TV
3900 Harry Hines Blvd.
Dallas, TX 75219
214–521–3900

WFAA–TV (ABC)
606 Young St.
Dallas, TX 75202
214–748–9631

KFWD (Telemundo)
3000 W. Story Rd.
Irving, TX 75038
214–637–5200

KTVT
5233 Bridge St.
Fort Worth, TX 76113
817–451–1111

KXAS–TV
3900 Barnett
Fort Worth, TX 76113
817–536–5555

9. Detroit, MI

WDIV–TV
550 W. Lafayette Blvd.
Detroit, MI 48231
313–222–0444

WGPR–TV
3146 E. Jefferson Ave.
Detroit, MI 48207
313–259–8862

WJBK–TV (CBS)
Box 2000
Southfield, MI 48037
313–557–2000

WKBD (Fox)
26905 W. Eleven Mile Rd.
Southfield, MI 48037
313–350–5050

WXON
27777 Franklin Rd., Ste. 1220
Southfield, MI 48034
313–355–2900

WXYZ–TV (ABC)
20777 W. Ten Mile Rd.
Southfield, MI 48037
313–827–7777

10. Atlanta, GA

WAGA–TV (CBS)
1551 Briarcliff Rd. NE
Atlanta, GA 30306
404–875–5555

WGNX
1810 Briarcliff Rd. NE
Atlanta, GA 30329
404–325–4646

WSB–TV (ABC)
1601 W. Peachtree St. NE
Atlanta, GA 30309
404–897–7000

WXIA–TV (NBC)
1611 W. Peachtree St. NE
Atlanta, GA 30309
404–892–1611

11. Houston, TX

KHOU–TV (CBS)
1945 Allen Pkwy.
Houston, TX 77019
713–526–1111

KHTV (independent)
7700 Westpark Dr.
Houston, TX 77063
713–781–3939

KPRC–TV (NBC)
Box 2222
Houston, TX 77252
713–771–4631

KRIV (Fox)
3935 Westheimer Rd.
Houston, TX 77227
713–626–2610

KTRK–TV (ABC)
3310 Bissonnet
Houston, TX 77005
713–666–0713

12. Cleveland, OH

WEWS (ABC)
3001 Euclid Ave.
Cleveland, OH 44115
216–431–5555

WJW–TV (CBS)
5800 S. Marginal Rd.
Cleveland, OH 44103
216–431–8888

WKYC–TV (NBC)
1403 E. Sixth St.
Cleveland, OH 44114
216–344–3333

WQHS
2861 W. Ridgewood Dr.
Parma, OH 44134
216–888–0061

WUAB
8443 Day Dr.
Cleveland, OH 44129
216–845–6043

13. Seattle–Tacoma, WA

KING–TV (NBC)
333 Dexter Ave. North
Seattle, WA 98124
206–448–5555

KIRO–TV (CBS)
2807 Third Ave.
Seattle, WA 98111
206–728–7777

KOMO–TV (ABC)
100 Fourth Ave. North
Seattle, WA 98109
206–443–4000

KSTW
Box 11411
Tacoma, WA 98411
206–572–5789

14. Tampa–St. Petersburg, FL

WFLA
905 E. Jackson St.
Tampa, FL 33602
813–228–8888

WTOG
365 105th Terr. NE
St. Petersburg, FL 33716
813–576–4444

WTSP (ABC)
11450 Gandy Blvd.
St. Petersburg, FL 33702
813–577–1010

WTVT (CBS)
3213 W. Kennedy Blvd.
Tampa, FL 33609
813–876–1313

15. Minneapolis–St. Paul, MN

KARE (NBC)
8811 Olson Memorial Hwy.
Minneapolis, MN 55427
612–546–1111

KITN–TV (Fox)
7325 Aspen Ln. North
Minneapolis, MN 55428
612–424–2929

KMSP–TV (independent)
6975 York Ave. South
Minneapolis, MN 55435
612–926–9999

KSTP–TV (ABC)
3415 University Ave.
St. Paul, MN 55114
612–646–5555

KTMA
1640 Como Ave.
St. Paul, MN 55108
612–646–2300

WCCO–TV (CBS)
90 S. 11th St.
Minneapolis, MN 55403
612–339–4444

16. Miami–Ft. Lauderdale, FL

WCIX (CBS)
8900 N.W. 18th Terr.
Miami, FL 33172
305–593–0606

WPLG (ABC)
3900 Biscayne Blvd.
Miami, FL 33137
305–576–1010

WSVN (Fox)
1401 79th St., Causeway
Miami, FL 33141
305–751–6692

WTVJ (NBC)
315 N. Miami Ave.
Miami, FL 33128
305–379–4444

17. Pittsburgh, PA

KDKA–TV (CBS)
One Gateway Ctr.
Pittsburgh, PA 15222
412–392–2200

WPXI (NBC)
11 Television Hill
Pittsburgh, PA 15230
412–237–1100

WTAE–TV (ABC)
400 Ardmore Blvd.
Pittsburgh, PA 15221
412–242–4300

18. St. Louis, MO

KMOV (CBS)
One Memorial Dr.
St. Louis, MO 63102
314–621–4444

KPLR–TV
4935 Lindell Blvd.
St. Louis, MO 63108
314–367–7211

KSDK (NBC)
1000 Market St.
St. Louis, MO 63101
314–421–5055

KTVI (ABC)
5915 Berthold Ave.
St. Louis, MO 63110
314–647–2222

19. Sacramento–Stockton, CA

KCRA–TV (NBC)
3 Television Cir.
Sacramento, CA 95814
916–446–3333

KCSO (Univision)
Box 3689
Modesto, CA 95352
209–578–1900

KOVR (ABC)
2713 KOVR Dr.
West Sacramento, CA 95605
916–374–1313

KRBK–TV
500 Media Pl.
Sacramento, CA 95815
916–929–0300

KTXL (Fox)
4655 Fruitridge Rd.
Sacramento, CA 95820
916–454–4422

KXTV (CBS)
400 Broadway
Sacramento, CA 95818
916–441–2345

20. Phoenix, AZ

KPHO–TV
4016 N. Black Canyon
Phoenix, AZ 85017
602–264–1000

KPNX (NBC)
1101 N. Central Ave.
Phoenix, AZ 85004
602–257–1212

KTSP–TV (CBS)
511 W. Adams St.
Phoenix, AZ 85003
602–257–1234

KTVK (ABC)
3435 N. 16th St.
Phoenix, AZ 85016
602–263–3333

KTVW–TV (Univision)
3019 E. Southern Ave.
Phoenix, AZ 85040
602–243–3333

21. Denver, CO

KCNC–TV (NBC)
Box 5012
Denver, CO 80217
303–861–4444

KMGH–TV (CBS)
123 Speer Blvd.
Denver, CO 80203
303–832–7777

KUSA–TV (ABC)
500 Speer Blvd.
Denver, CO 80203
303–871–9999

KWGN–TV (independent)
6160 S. Wabash Way
Englewood, CO 80111
303–740–2222

22. Baltimore, MD

WBAL–TV (CBS)
3800 Hooper Ave.
Baltimore, MD 21211
410–467–3000

WBFF (Fox)
2000 W. 41st St.
Baltimore, MD 21211
410–467–4545

WJZ–TV (ABC)
TV Hill
Baltimore, MD 21211
410–466–0013

WMAR–TV (NBC)
64009 York Rd.
Baltimore, MD 21212
410–377–2222

WMPB (noncommercial)
11767 Owings Mills Blvd.
Owings Mill, MD 21117
410–356–5600

23. Orlando–Daytona Beach–Melbourne, FL

WAYO
944 Sea Breeze Blvd., Ste. 940
Daytona Beach, FL 32018
904–238–0026

WCPX–TV (CBS)
4466 John Young Pkwy.
Orlando, FL 32804
407–291–6000

WESH (NBC)
211 N. Ridgewood Ave.
Daytona Beach, FL 32115
904–226–2222

WFTV
490 E. South St.
Orlando, FL 32801
407–841–9000

WOFL (Fox)
35 Skyline Dr.
Lake Mary, FL 32746
407–644–3535

24. Hartford–New Haven, CT

WFSB (CBS)
3 Constitution Plaza
Hartford, CT 06103
203–728–3333

WTIC–TV (Fox)
One Corporate Ctr.
Hartford, CT 06103
203–527–6161

WVIT (NBC)
1422 New Britain Ave.
West Hartford, CT 06110
203–521–3030

WTNH–TV (ABC)
Box 1859
New Haven, CT 06508
203–784–8888

WTWS
216 Broad St.
New London, CT 06320
203–444–2626

25. San Diego, CA

KFMB–TV (CBS)
7677 Engineer Rd.
San Diego, CA 92111
619–571–8888

KGTV (ABC)
Box 85347
San Diego, CA 92186
619–237–1010

KNSD (NBC)
8330 Engineer Rd.
San Diego, CA 92171
619–279–3939

KUSI–TV
4575 Viewridge Ave.
San Diego, CA 92123
619–571–5151

XEWT–TV (Tijuana, Mexico)
8253 Ronson Rd.
San Ysidro, CA 92073
706–684–5185

26. Indianapolis, IN

WISH–TV (CBS)
1950 N. Meridian St.
Indianapolis, IN 46207
317–923–8888

WRTV (ABC)
1330 N. Meridian St.
Indianapolis, IN 46202
317–635–9788

WTHR (NBC)
1000 N. Meridian St.
Indianapolis, IN 46204
317–636–1313

WXIN (Fox)
1440 N. Meridian St.
Indianapolis, IN 46202
317–632–5900

27. Portland, OR

KATU (ABC)
2153 N.E. Sandy Blvd.
Portland, OR 97232
503–231–4222

KGW–TV (NBC)
1501 S.W. Jefferson St.
Portland, OR 97201
503–226–5000

KOIN–TV (CBS)
222 S.W. Columbia St.
Portland, OR 97201
503–464–0600

KPTV
Box 3401
Portland, OR 97208
503–222–9921

28. Milwaukee, WI

WISN–TV (ABC)
Box 402
Milwaukee, WI 53201
414–342–8812

WITI–TV (CBS)
9001 N. Green Bay Rd.
Milwaukee, WI 53217
414–355–6666

WMVS (noncommercial)
1036 N. Eighth St.
Milwaukee, WI 53233
414–271–1036

WTMJ–TV (NBC)
720 E. Capitol Dr.
Milwaukee, WI 53201
414–332–9611

WVTV
4041 N. 35th St.
Milwaukee, WI 53216
414–442–7050

29. Kansas City, MO

KCTV (CBS)
4500 Shawnee Mission Pkwy.
Fairway, KS 66205
913–677–5555

KMBC–TV (ABC)
1049 Central
Kansas City, MO 64105
816–221–9999

KSHB–TV (Fox)
4720 Oak St.
Kansas City, MO 64112
816–753–4141

WDAF–TV (NBC)
Signal Hill
Kansas City, MO 64108
816–753–4567

30. Charlotte, NC

WBTV (CBS)
One Julian Price Pl.
Charlotte, NC 28208
704–374–3500

WCCB (Fox)
One TV Pl.
Charlotte, NC 28205
704–372–1800

WCNC–TV (NBC)
1001 Wood Ridge Ctr. Dr.
Charlotte, NC 28217
704–329–3636

WSOC–TV (ABC)
1901 N. Tryon St.
Charlotte, NC 28206
704–335–4999

31. Cincinnati, OH

WCPO–TV (CBS)
500 Central Ave.
Cincinnati, OH 45202
513–721–9900

WKRC–TV (ABC)
1906 Highland Ave.
Cincinnati, OH 45219
513–763–5500

WLWT (NBC)
140 W. Ninth St.
Cincinnati, OH 45202
513–352–5000

WXIC–TV (Fox)
10490 Taconic Terr.
Cincinnati, OH 45215
513–772–1919

32. Raleigh–Durham, NC

WPTF–TV (NBC)
3012 Highwoods Blvd.
Durham, NC 27604
919–876–0674

WRAL–TV (CBS)
2619 Western Blvd.
Raleigh, NC 20606
919–821–8555

WRMY
126 N. Washington St.
Rocky Mount, NC 27801
919–985–2447

WTVD
Box 2009
Durham, NC 27702
919–683–1111

33. Nashville, TN

WKRN–TV (ABC)
441 Murfreesboro Rd.
Nashville, TN 37210
615–259–2200

WSMV (NBC)
5700 Knob Rd.
Nashville, TN 37209
615–749–2244

WTVF (CBS)
474 James Robertson Pkwy.
Nashville, TN 37219
615–244–5000

34. Columbus, OH

WBNS–TV (CBS)
770 Twin Rivers Dr.
Columbus, OH 43215
614–460–3700

WCMH (NBC)
3165 Olentangy River Rd.
Columbus, OH 43202
614–263–4444

WSYX
1261 Dublin Rd.
Columbus, OH 43216
614–481–6666

WWAT
1281 River Rd.
Chillicothe, OH 45601
614–775–3578

35. Greenville, SC–Spartanburg, SC–Asheville, NC

WLOS (ABC)
288 Macon Ave.
Asheville, NC 28804
704–255–0013

WSPA–TV (CBS)
250 International Dr.
Spartanburg, SC 29304
803–576–7777

WYFF–TV (NBC)
505 Rutherford St.
Greenville, SC 29602
803–242–4404

36. Grand Rapids–Kalamazoo–Battle Creek, MI

WUHQ–TV (ABC)
5200 W. Dickman Rd.
Battle Creek, MI 49016
616–968–9341

WOTV (NBC)
Box B
Grand Rapids, MI 49501
616–456–8888

WZZM–TV (ABC)
645 Three Mile Rd. NW
Grand Rapids, MI 49504
616–784–4200

WGVK (noncommercial)
301 W. Fulton St.
Grand Rapids, MI 49504
616–771–6666

WWMT (CBS)
590 W. Maple St.
Kalamazoo, MI 49008
616–388–3333

37. Buffalo, NY

WGRZ–TV (NBC)
259 Delaware Ave.
Buffalo, NY 14202
716–856–1414

WIVB–TV (CBS)
2077 Elmwood Ave.
Buffalo, NY 14207
716–874–4410

WKBW–TV (ABC)
7 Broadcast Plaza
Buffalo, NY 14202
716–845–6100

38. Norfolk–Portsmouth–Newport News–Hampton, VA

WAVY–TV (NBC)
300 Wavy St.
Portsmouth, VA 23704
804–393–1010

WTKR–TV (CBS)
720 Boush St.
Norfolk, VA 23510
804–446–1000

WVEC–TV (ABC)
613 Woodis Ave.
Norfolk, VA 23510
804–625–1313

WGNT
1318 Spratley St.
Portsmouth, VA 23704
804–393–2501

39. San Antonio, TX

KENS–TV (CBS)
5400 Fredericksburg Rd.
San Antonio, TX 78299
512–366–5000

KMOL–TV (NBC)
1031 Navarro Rd.
San Antonio, TX 78205
512–226–4444

KSAT–TV (ABC)
1408 N. Saint Mary's St.
San Antonio, TX 78215
512–351–1200

KVDA (Telemundo)
6234 San Pedro Rd.
San Antonio, TX 78216
512–340–8860

40. New Orleans, LA

WDSU–TV (NBC)
520 Royal St.
New Orleans, LA 70130
504–527–0666

WVUE (ABC)
1025 S. Jefferson Davis Pkwy.
New Orleans, LA 70125
504–486–6161

WWL–TV (CBS)
1024 N. Rampart St.
New Orleans, LA 70116
504–529–4444

41. Salt Lake City, UT

KSL–TV (CBS)
Broadcast House
Salt Lake City, UT 84110
801–575–5500

KTVX (ABC)
1760 Fremont Dr.
Salt Lake City, UT 84104
801–972–1776

KUTV
2185 South, 3600 West
Salt Lake City, UT 84119
801–973–3000

42. Memphis, TN

WHBQ–TV (ABC)
485 S. Highland Ave.
Memphis, TN 38111
901–320–1313

WMC–TV (NBC)
1960 Union Ave.
Memphis, TN 38104
901–726–0555

WREG–TV (CBS)
803 Channel 3 Dr.
Memphis, TN 38103
901–577–0100

43. Providence, RI–
New Bedford, MA

WJAR (NBC)
111 Dorrance St.
Providence, RI 02903
401–455–9100

WLNE (CBS)
10 Orms St.
Providence, RI 02904
401–751–6666

WPRI–TV (ABC)
25 Catamore Blvd.
East Providence, RI 02914
401–438–7200

**44. Harrisburg–Lancaster–
Lebanon–York, PA**

WHP–TV (CBS)
3300 N. Sixth St.
Harrisburg, PA 17110
717–238–2100

WHTM–TV (ABC)
3235 Hoffman St.
Harrisburg, PA 17110
717–236–2727

WITF–TV (noncommercial)
1982 Locust Ln.
Harrisburg, PA 17109
717–236–6000

WGAL (NBC)
1300 Columbia Ave.
Lancaster, PA 17604
717–393–5851

WLYH–TV (CBS)
Television Hill
Lebanon, PA 17042
717–273–4551

45. Oklahoma City, OK

KETA (noncommercial)
7403 N. Kelley
Oklahoma City, OK 73113
405–848–8501

KFOR–TV (NBC)
444 E. Britton Rd.
Oklahoma City, OK 73114
405–478–1212

KOCO–TV (ABC)
1300 E. Britton Rd.
Oklahoma City, OK 73113
405–478–3000

KOKH–TV
1228 E. Wilshire Blvd.
Oklahoma City, OK 73111
405–843–2525

KWTV (CBS)
7401 N. Kelley Ave.
Oklahoma City, OK 73111
405–843–6641

**46. West Palm Beach–
Fort Pierce–Vero Beach, FL**

WTVX
Box 3434
Fort Pierce, FL 34954
305–464–3434

WPBF (ABC)
3970 RCA Blvd., Ste. 7007
Palm Beach Gardens, FL 33410
407–694–2525

WPEC (CBS)
Box 24612
West Palm Beach, FL 33416
407–844–1212

WPTV (NBC)
622 N. Flagler Dr.
West Palm Beach, FL 33401
407–655–5455

**47. Wilkes-Barre–
Scranton, PA**

WBRE–TV (NBC)
62 S. Franklin St.
Wilkes-Barre, PA 18773
717–823–2828

WNEP–TV (ABC)
16 Montage Mountain Rd.
Moosic, PA 18507
717–346–7474

WYOU (CBS)
415 Lackawanna Ave.
Scranton, PA 18503
717–961–2222

**48. Greensboro–
High Point–
Winston-Salem, NC**

WAAP
Bass Mountain Rd.
Snow Camp, NC 27349
919–376–6016

WFMY–TV (CBS)
1615 Phillips Ave.
Greensboro, NC 27405
919–379–9369

WGHP–TV (ABC)
2005 Francis St.
High Point, NC 27263
919–841–8888

WXII (NBC)
700 Coliseum Dr.
Winston-Salem, NC 27116
919–721–9944

49. Albuquerque–Santa Fe, NM

KGGM–TV (CBS)
Box 1294
Albuquerque, NM 87103
505–243–2285

KGSW–TV (Fox)
1377 University Blvd. NE
Albuquerque, NM 87102
505–842–1414

KLUZ–TV (Univision)
2725 F Broadbent Pkwy. NE
Albuquerque, NM 87107
505–344–5589

KOAT–TV (ABC)
3801 Carlisle NE
Albuquerque, NM 87107
505–884–7777

KOB–TV (NBC)
Box 1351
Albuquerque, NM 87103
505–243–4411

KCHF–TV (independent)
216 TV E. Frontage Rd.
Santa Fe, NM 87505
505–473–1111

KKTO–TV (independent)
1311 Calle Nava
Santa Fe, NM 87501
505–982–2422

50. Louisville, KY

WAVE (NBC)
725 S. Floyd St.
Louisville, KY 40203
502–585–2201

WDRB–TV (Fox)
Independence Sq.
Louisville, KY 40203
502–584–6441

WHAS–TV (ABC)
520 W. Chestnut St.
Louisville, KY 40202
502–582–7840

WLKY–TV (CBS)
1918 Mellwood Ave.
Louisville, KY 40206
502–893–3671

51. Birmingham, AL

WBMG (CBS)
2075 Goldencrest Dr.
Birmingham, AL 35209
205–322–4200

WBRC–TV (ABC)
1720 Valley View Dr.
Birmingham, AL 35209
205–322–6666

WVTM–TV (NBC)
Box 10502
Birmingham, AL 35202
205–933–1313

**52. Albany–Schenectady–
Troy, NY**

WNYT (NBC)
15 N. Pearl St.
Albany, NY 12204
518–436–4791

WRGB (CBS)
1400 Balltown Rd.
Schenectady, NY 12309
518–346–6666

WTEN (ABC)
341 Northern Blvd.
Albany, NY 12204
518–436–4822

53. Dayton, OH

WDTN (ABC)
4595 S. Dixie Ave.
Dayton, OH 45439
513–293–2101

WHIO–TV (CBS)
1414 Wilmington Ave.
Dayton, OH 45420
513–259–2111

WKEF (NBC)
1731 Soldiers Home Rd.
Dayton, OH 45418
513–263–2662

WPTD (noncommercial)
110 S. Jefferson St.
Dayton, OH 45402
513–220–1600

WTJC
2675 Dayton Rd.
Springfield, OH 45506
513–323–4026

54. Richmond, VA

WRIC–TV (ABC)
Arboretum Pl.
Richmond, VA 23236
804–330–8888

WTVR–TV (CBS)
3301 W. Broad St.
Richmond, VA 23230
804–254–3600

WWBT (NBC)
5710 Midlothian Tpk.
Richmond, VA 23255
804–230–2793

55. Jacksonville, FL

WJKS (ABC)
9117 Hogan Rd.
Jacksonville, FL 32216
904–641–1700

WJXT (CBS)
4 Broadcast Pl.
Jacksonville, FL 32207
904–399–4000

WNFT
1 Independent Dr.
Jacksonville, FL 32202
904–355–4747

WTLV (NBC)
1070 E. Adams St.
Jacksonville, FL 32202
904–354–1212

56. Charleston–Huntington, WV

WCHS–TV (ABC)
1301 Piedmont Rd.
Charleston, WV 25301
304–346–5358

WOWK–TV (CBS)
555 Fifth Ave.
Huntington, WV 25701
304–525–7661

WSAZ–TV (NBC)
645 Fifth Ave.
Huntington, WV 25721
304–697–4780

57. Fresno–Visalia, CA

KAIL
1590 Alluvial Ave.
Clovis, CA 93612
209–299–9753

KFSN–TV (ABC)
1777 G St.
Fresno, CA 93706
209–442–1170

KFTV (Univision)
3239 W. Ashlan Ave.
Fresno, CA 93722
209–222–2121

KJEO (CBS)
4880 N. First St.
Fresno, CA 93726
209–222–2411

KMPH (Fox)
5111 E. McKinley Ave.
Fresno, CA 93727
209–255–2600

KSEE (NBC)
5035 E. McKinley Ave.
Fresno, CA 93727
209–454–2424

58. Little Rock–Pine Bluff, AR

KARK–TV (NBC)
Box 748
Little Rock, AR 72203
501–376–4444

KATV
401 S. Main
Little Rock, AR 72201
501–324–7777

KTHV (CBS)
720 Izard St.
Little Rock, AR 72202
501–376–1111

59. Tulsa, OK

KJRH (NBC)
3701 S. Peoria
Tulsa, OK 74105
918–743–2222

KOKI–TV (Fox)
7422 E. 46th Pl.
Tulsa, OK 74145
918–622–2300

KOTV (CBS)
302 S. Frankfort
Tulsa, OK 74101
918–582–6666

KTUL–TV (ABC)
Box 8
Tulsa, OK 74101
918–446–3351

60. Flint–Saginaw–Bay City, MI

WEYI–TV (CBS)
2225 W. Willard Rd.
Clio, MI 48420
517–755–0525

WJRT–TV (ABC)
2302 Lapeer Rd.
Flint, MI 48503
313–233–3130

WNEM–TV (NBC)
107 N. Franklin St.
Saginaw, MI 48606
517–755–8191

61. Wichita–Hutchinson, KS

KLBY
990 S. Range St.
Colby, KS 67701
913–462–8644

KBSH–TV
2300 Hall St.
Hays, KS 67601
913–625–5277

KOOD (noncommercial)
Bunker Hill
Hays, KS 67626
913–483–6990

KAKE–TV (ABC)
1500 N. West St.
Wichita, KS 67203
316–943–4221

KSNW (NBC)
833 N. Main
Wichita, KS 67203
316–265–3333

KWCH–TV (CBS)
Box 12
Wichita, KS 67201
316–838–1212

62. Mobile, AL–Pensacola, FL

WALA–TV (NBC)
210 Government St.
Mobile, AL 36602
205–434–1010

WEAR–TV (ABC)
Box 12278
Pensacola, FL 32581
904–456–3333

WKRG–TV (CBS)
555 Broadcast Dr.
Mobile, AL 36606
205–479–5555

63. Knoxville, TN

WINT–TV
Box 608
Crossville, TN 38555
615–484–1220

WATE–TV (ABC)
1306 N.E. Broadway
Knoxville, TN 37917
615–637–6666

WBIR–TV (NBC)
1513 Hutchison Ave.
Knoxville, TN 37917
615–637–1010

WKXT–TV (CBS)
Box 59088
Knoxville, TN 37950
615–689–8000

64. Toledo, OH

WNWO–TV (ABC)
300 S. Byrne Rd.
Toledo, OH 43615
419–535–0024

WTOL–TV (CBS)
730 N. Summit St.
Toledo, OH 43695
419–248–1111

WTVG–TV (NBC)
4247 Dorr St.
Toledo, OH 43607
419–531–1313

65. Roanoke–Lynchburg, VA

WDBJ (CBS)
2001 Colonial Ave.
Roanoke, VA 24015
703–344–7000

WSET–TV (ABC)
2320 Langhorne Rd.
Lynchburg, VA 24501
804–528–1313

WSLS–TV (NBC)
Box 2161
Roanoke, VA 24009
703–981–9110

66. Syracuse, NY

WIXT–TV (ABC)
Box 9
East Syracuse, NY 13057
315–446–4780

WSTM–TV (NBC)
1030 James St.
Syracuse, NY 13203
315–474–5000

WTVH–TV (CBS)
980 James St.
Syracuse, NY 13203
315–425–5555

67. Austin, TX

KBVO (Fox)
10700 Metric Blvd.
Austin, TX 78758
512–835–0042

KTBC–TV (CBS)
119 E. Tenth St.
Austin, TX 78701
512–476–7777

KVUE–TV (ABC)
3201 Steck Ave.
Austin, TX 78758
512–459–6521

KXAN–TV (NBC)
Box 490
Austin, TX 78767
512–476–3636

68. Green Bay–Appleton, WI

WBAY–TV (CBS)
115 S. Jefferson
Green Bay, WI 54301
414–432–3331

WFRV–TV (ABC)
1181 E. Mason St.
Green Bay, WI 54307
414–437–5411

WLUK–TV (NBC)
787 Lombardi Ave.
Green Bay, WI 54307
414–494–8711

69. Shreveport, LA

KSLA–TV (CBS)
1812 Fairfield Ave.
Shreveport, LA 71104
318–222–1212

KTAL–TV (NBC)
3150 N. Market St.
Shreveport, LA 71007
318–425–2422

KTBS–TV (ABC)
312 E. Kings Hwy.
Shreveport, LA 71104
318–861–5800

70. Honolulu, HI

KGBM (CBS)
1534 Kapiolani Blvd.
Honolulu, HI 96814
808–944–5200

KHON–TV (NBC)
1116 Auahi St.
Honolulu, HI 96814
808–531–8585

KITV (ABC)
1290 Ala Moana Blvd.
Honolulu, HI 96814
808–545–4444

71. Lexington, KY

WYMT–TV (CBS)
U.S. 15 Bypass
Hazard, KY 41702
606–436–5757

WKYT–TV (CBS)
2851 Winchester Rd.
Lexington, KY 40509
606–299–0411

WLEX–TV (NBC)
1065 Russell Cave Rd.
Lexington, KY 40505
606–255–4404

WTVQ–TV (ABC)
2940 Bryant Rd.
Lexington, KY 40509
606–233–3600

72. Rochester, NY

WHEC–TV (NBC)
191 East Ave.
Rochester, NY 14604
716–546–5670

WOKR–TV (ABC)
4225 W. Henrietta Rd.
Rochester, NY 14623
716–334–8700

WROC–TV (CBS)
201 Humboldt St.
Rochester, NY 14610
716–288–8400

WUHF–TV (Fox)
360 East Ave.
Rochester, NY 14604
716–232–3700

73. Des Moines, IA

KCCI–TV (CBS)
888 Ninth St.
Des Moines, IA 50309
515–247–8888

KDSM–TV (Fox)
4023 Fleur Dr.
Des Moines, IA 50321
515–287–1717

WHCO–TV (NBC)
1801 Grand Ave.
Des Moines, IA 50309
515–242–3500

WOI–TV (ABC)
WOI Building
Ames, IA 50011
515–294–5555

74. Portland–Auburn, ME

WCSH–TV (NBC)
One Congress Sq.
Portland, ME 04101
207–828–6666

WGME–TV (CBS)
Box 1731
Portland, ME 04104
207–797–9330

WMTW–TV (ABC)
99 Danville Cor Rd.
Auburn, ME 04210
207–775–1800

75. Omaha, NE

KETV (ABC)
2665 Douglas St.
Omaha, NE 68131–2699
402–345–7777

KMTV (CBS)
10714 Mockingbird Dr.
Omaha, NE 68127
402–592–3333

KPTM (Fox)
4625 Farnam St.
Omaha, NE 68132
402–558–4200

WOWT (NBC)
3501 Farnam St.
Omaha, NE 68131
402–346–6666

**76. Paducah, KY–
Cape Girardeau, MO–
Harrisburg, IL–Mt. Vernon, IL**

WPSD–TV (NBC)
100 Television Ln.
Paducah, KY 42003
502–442–8214

KFVS–TV (CBS)
310 Broadway
Cape Girardeau, MO 63701
314–335–1212

WSIL–TV (ABC)
21 Country Aire Rd.
Carterville, IL 62918
618–985–2333

77. Champaign–Springfield–Decatur, IL

WCIA (CBS)
509 S. Neil
Champaign, IL 61824
217–356–8333

WICD (NBC)
250 County Fair Dr.
Champaign, IL 61821
217–351–8500

WAND (ABC)
904 Southside Dr.
Decatur, IL 62521
217–424–2500

WFHL
2510 Parkway Ct.
Decatur, IL 62526
217–428–2323

WCEE
125 N. 11th St.
Mt. Vernon, IL 62864
618–822–6900

WICS (NBC)
2680 E. Cook St.
Springfield, IL 62703
217–753–5620

78. Las Vegas, NV

KLAS–TV (CBS)
3228 Channel 8 Dr.
Las Vegas, NV 89109
702–792–8888

KLVX (noncommercial)
4210 Channel 10 Dr.
Las Vegas, NV 89119
702–737–1010

KTNV (ABC)
3355 Valley View Blvd.
Las Vegas, NV 89102
702–876–1313

KVBC (NBC)
1500 Foremaster Ln.
Las Vegas, NV 89101
702–642–3333

79. Spokane, WA

KHQ–TV (NBC)
4202 S. Regal
Spokane, WA 99223
509–448–6000

KREM–TV (CBS)
4103 S. Regal
Spokane, WA 99203
509–448–2000

KXLY–TV (ABC)
W. 500 Boone Ave.
Spokane, WA 99201
509–328–9084

80. Springfield, MO

KOLR–TV (CBS)
2650 E. Division St.
Springfield, MO 65803
417–862–1010

KSPR (ABC)
1359 St. Louis St.
Springfield, MO 65802
417–831–1333

KYTV (NBC)
999 W. Sunshine
Springfield, MO 65807
417–868–3800

81. Tucson, AZ

KGUN (ABC)
7280 E. Rosewood St.
Tucson, AZ 85710
602–722–5486

KOLD–TV (CBS)
115 W. Drachman St.
Tucson, AZ 85705
602–624–2511

KUAT–TV (noncommercial)
Univ. of Arizona
Tucson, AZ 85721
602–621–5828

KVOA–TV (NBC)
209 W. Elm St.
Tucson, AZ 85705
602–792–2270

82. Chattanooga, TN

WDEF–TV (CBS)
3300 Broad St.
Chattanooga, TN 37408
615–267–0009

WRCB–TV (NBC)
900 Whitehall Rd.
Chattanooga, TN 37405
615–267–5412

WTVC (ABC)
410 W. Sixth St.
Chattanooga, TN 37402
615–756–5500

83. South Bend–Elkhart, IN

WNDU–TV (NBC)
Box 1616
South Bend, IN 46634
219–239–1616

WSBT–TV (CBS)
300 W. Jefferson Blvd.
South Bend, IN 46601
219–233–3141

WSJV (ABC)
Box 1646
South Bend, IN 46515
219–293–8616

**84. Cedar Rapids–
Waterloo–Dubuque, IA**

KCRG–TV (ABC)
Box 816
Cedar Rapids, IA 52406
319–398–8422

KDUB–TV (ABC)
One Cycare Plaza
Dubuque, IA 52001
319–556–4040

KGAN (CBS)
Box 3131
Cedar Rapids, IA 52406
319–395–9060

KWWL (NBC)
500 E. Fourth St.
Waterloo, IA 50703
319–291–1200

85. Madison, WI

WISC–TV (CBS)
7025 Raymond Rd.
Madison, WI 53719
608–271–4321

WKOW–TV (ABC)
Box 100
Madison, WI 53701
608–274–1234

WMTV (NBC)
615 Forward Dr.
Madison, WI 53711
608–274–1515

86. Fort Myers–Naples, FL

WBBH–TV (NBC)
3719 Central Ave.
Fort Myers, FL 33911
813–939–2020

WEVU (ABC)
3451 Bonita Bay Blvd.
Bonita Springs, FL 33923
813–332–0076

WINK–TV (CBS)
2824 Palm Beach Blvd.
Fort Myers, FL 33916
813–334–1131

WNPL–TV
840 Goodlette Rd. N.
Naples, FL 33940
813–261–4600

**87. Burlington, VT–
Plattsburgh, NY**

WPTZ (NBC)
Old Moffitt Rd.
Plattsburgh, NY 12901
518–561–5555

WCAX–TV (CBS)
Box 608
Burlington, VT 05402
802–658–6300

WVNY (ABC)
100 Market Sq.
Burlington, VT 05401
802–658–8022

WNNE–TV (NBC)
Box 1310
White River Junction, VT 05001
802–295–3100

**88. Davenport, IA–
Rock Island, IL–Moline, IL**

KLJB–TV (Fox)
937 E. 53rd St., Ste. D
Davenport, IA 52807
319–386–1818

KWQC–TV (NBC)
805 Brady St.
Davenport, IA 52808
319–383–7000

WHBF–TV (CBS)
231 18th St.
Rock Island, IL 61201
309–786–5441

WQAD–TV (ABC)
3003 Park 16th St.
Moline, IL 61265
309–764–8888

89. Columbia, SC

WIS–TV (NBC)
1111 Bull St.
Columbia, SC 29201
803–799–1010

WLTX (CBS)
Drawer M
Columbia, SC 29250
803–776–3600

WOLO–TV (ABC)
5807 Shakespeare Rd.
Columbia, SC 29240
803–754–7525

WRLK–TV (noncommercial)
2712 Millwood Ave.
Columbia, SC 29205
803–737–3200

90. Huntsville–Decatur, AL

WAAY–TV (ABC)
1000 Monte Sano Blvd.
Huntsville, AL 35801
205–533–3131

WAFF (NBC)
Box 2116
Huntsville, AL 35804
205–533–4848

WHNT–TV (CBS)
960 Monte Sano Blvd.
Huntsville, AL 35801
205–539–1919

WOWL–TV (NBC)
840 Cypress Mid Rd.
Florence, AL 35630
205–767–1515

91. Jackson, MS

WAPT (ABC)
One Channel 16 Way
Jackson, MS 39209
601–922–1607

WDBD (Fox)
7440 Channel 16 Way
Jackson, MS 39289
601–922–1234

WJTV (CBS)
1820 TV Rd.
Jackson, MS 39204
601–372–6311

WLBT (NBC)
715 S. Jefferson St.
Jackson, MS 39205
601–948–3333

WNTZ
625 Beltline Hwy.
Natchez, MS 39120
601–442–4800

92. Tri–Cities, TN–VA

WJHL–TV (CBS)
Box 1130
Johnson City, TN 37601
615–926–2151

WKPT–TV (ABC)
222 Commerce St.
Kingsport, TN 37660
615–246–9578

WCYB–TV (NBC)
101 Lee St.
Bristol, VA 24203
703–669–4161

93. Johnstown–Altoona, PA

WATM–TV (ABC)
1450 Scalp Ave.
Johnstown, PA 15904
814–266–8088

WTAJ–TV (CBS)
Box 10, Commerce Pk.
Altoona, PA 16603
814–944–2031

WJAC–TV (NBC)
Hickory Ln.
Johnstown, PA 15905
814–255–7600

WWCP–TV (Fox)
1450 Scalp Ave.
Johnstown, PA 15904
814–266–8088

94. Youngstown, OH

WFMJ–TV (NBC)
101 W. Boardman St.
Youngstown, OH 44503
216–744–8611

WKBN–TV (CBS)
3930 Sunset Blvd.
Youngstown, OH 44501
216–782–1144

WYTV (ABC)
3800 Shady Run Rd.
Youngstown, Ohio 44502
216–783–2930

95. Evansville, IN

WEHT (CBS)
800 Marywood Dr.
Henderson, KY 42420
812–424–9215

WFIE–TV (NBC)
1115 Mount Auburn Rd.
Evansville, IN 47712
812–426–1414

WTVW (ABC)
477 Carpenter St.
Evansville, IN 47708
812–422–1121

96. Baton Rouge, LA

WAFB (CBS)
Box 2671
Baton Rouge, LA 70821
504–383–9999

WBRZ (ABC)
1650 Highland Rd.
Baton Rouge, LA 70802
504–387–2222

WVLA (NBC)
5220 Essen Ln.
Baton Rouge, LA 70809
504–766–3233

97. Waco–Temple–Bryan, TX

KBTX–TV (CBS)
Drawer 3730
Bryan, TX 77805
409–846–7777

KWTX–TV (CBS)
6700 American Plaza
Waco, TX 76712
817–776–1330

KXXV (ABC)
1909 S. New Rd.
Waco, TX 76702
817–754–2525

KCEN–TV (NBC)
4716 W. Waco Dr.
Waco, TX 76710
817–773–6868

98. Lincoln–Hastings–Kearney, NE

KHAS–TV (NBC)
Box 578
Hastings, NE 68901
402–463–1321

KHGI–TV (ABC)
Box 220
Kearney, NE 68848
308–743–2494

KOLN (CBS)
Box 30350
Lincoln, NE 68503
402–467–4321

KSNB–TV
Box 220
Superior, NE 68848
308–743–2494

99. Springfield–Holyoke, MA

WGGB–TV (ABC)
1300 Liberty St.
Springfield, MA 01102
413–733–4040

WWLP (NBC)
Box 2210
Springfield, MA 01102
413–786–2200

**100. Colorado Springs–
Pueblo, CO**

KKTV (CBS)
3100 N. Nevada Ave.
Colorado Springs, CO 80907
719–634–2844

KOAA–TV (NBC)
530 Communications Cir.
Colorado Springs, CO 80905
719–544–5781

KRDO–TV (ABC)
399 S. Eighth St.
Colorado Springs, CO 80901
719–632–1515

101. El Paso, TX

KDBC–TV (CBS)
2201 Wyoming
El Paso, TX 79903
915–532–6551

KINT–TV (Univision)
5426 N. Mesa
El Paso, TX 79912
915–581–1126

KTSM–TV (NBC)
801 N. Oregon St.
El Paso, TX 79902
915–532–5421

KVIA–TV (ABC)
4140 Rio Bravo
El Paso, TX 79902
915–532–7777

XHIJ (Telemundo)
5925 Cromo
El Paso, TX 79912
915–833–4044

102. Fort Wayne, IN

WANE–TV (CBS)
2915 W. State Blvd.
Fort Wayne, IN 46801
219–424–1515

WFFT–TV (Fox)
3707 Hillegas Rd.
Fort Wayne, IN 46808
219–424–5555

WKJG–TV (NBC)
2633 W. State Blvd.
Fort Wayne, IN 46808
219–422–7474

WPTA (ABC)
3401 Butler Rd.
Fort Wayne, IN 48604
219–483–0584

103. Savannah, GA

WJCL (ABC)
10001 Abercorn St.
Savannah, GA 31406
912–925–0022

WSAV–TV (NBC)
Box 2429
Savannah, GA 31402
912–651–4300

WTOC–TV (CBS)
Box 8086
Savannah, GA 31412
912–234–1111

104. Lansing, MI

WLAJ–TV (ABC)
5815 S. Pennsylvania Ave.
Lansing, MI 48909
517–394–5300

WLNS–TV (CBS)
2820 E. Saginaw
Lansing, MI 48912
517–372–8282

WILX–TV (NBC)
500 American Rd.
Lansing, MI 48911
517–783–2621

105. Greenville–New Bern–Washington, NC

WCTI (ABC)
400 Glenburnie Dr.
New Bern, NC 28561
919–638–1212

WITN–TV (NBC)
Highway 17 South
Greenville, NC 27889
919–946–3131

WNCT–TV (CBS)
3221 Evans St.
Greenville, NC 27835
919–355–8500

106. Charleston, SC

WCBD–TV (ABC)
210 W. Coleman Blvd.
Mount Pleasant, SC 29464
803–884–2222

WCIV (NBC)
1558 Highway 703
Mount Pleasant, SC 29464
803–881–4444

WCSC–TV (CBS)
485 E. Bay St.
Charleston, SC 29402
803–723–8371

107. Sioux Falls–Mitchell, SD

KDLT (NBC)
3600 S. Westport Ave.
Mitchell, SD 57116
605–361–5555

KELO–TV (CBS)
Phillips at 13th
Sioux Falls, SD 57102
605–336–1100

KSFY–TV (ABC)
300 N. Dakota
Sioux Falls, SD 57102
605–336–1300

108. Fargo–Valley City, ND

KFME (noncommercial)
207 N. Fifth St.
Fargo, ND 58108
701–241–6900

KTHI–TV (NBC)
Box 1878
Fargo, ND 58107
701–237–5211

KXJB–TV (CBS)
4302 13th Ave. S.
Fargo, ND 58103
701–282–0444

WDAY–TV (ABC)
301 S. Eighth St.
Fargo, ND 58107
701–237–6500

109. Santa Barbara–San Luis Obispo, CA

KCOY–TV (CBS)
1211 W. McCay Ln.
Santa Maria, CA 93455
805–925–1200

KSBY–TV (NBC)
467 Hill St.
San Luis Obispo, CA 93401
805–541–6666

KEYT–TV (ABC)
Miramonte Dr.
Santa Barbara, CA 93109
805–965–8533

110. Montgomery, AL

WHOA–TV (ABC)
3251 Harrison Rd.
Montgomery, AL 36109
205–272–5331

WSFA (NBC)
10 E. Delano Ave.
Montgomery, AL 36105
205–281–2900

WAKA (CBS)
3020 East Blvd.
Selma, AL 36116
205–279–8787

111. Salinas–Monterey, CA

KCBA (Fox)
1550 Moffett St.
Salinas, CA 93905
408–422–3500

KMST (CBS)
2200 Garden Rd.
Monterey, CA 93940
408–649–0460

KSBW (NBC)
238 John St.
Salinas, CA 93901
408–758–8888

KSMS–TV (Univision)
67 Garden Ct.
Monterey, CA 93940
408–373–6767

112. Peoria–Bloomington, IL

WEEK–TV (NBC)
2907 Springfield Rd.
Peoria, IL 61611
309–698–2525

WHOI (ABC)
500 N. Stewart St.
Peoria, IL 61611
309–698–1919

WMBD–TV (CBS)
3131 N. University St.
Peoria, IL 61604
309–688–3131

113. Augusta, GA

WAGT (NBC)
905 Broad St.
Augusta, GA 30901
404–826–0026

WJBF (ABC)
Tenth & Reynolds Sts.
Augusta, GA 30901
404–722–6664

WRDW–TV (CBS)
1301 Georgia Ave.
North Augusta, SC 29841
803–278–1212

114. Harlingen–Weslaco–Brownsville, TX

KGBT–TV (CBS)
9201 W. Expressway 83
Harlingen, TX 78552
512–421–1444

KRGV–TV (ABC)
Box 5
Weslaco, TX 78596
512–968–5555

KVEO–TV (NBC)
394 N. Expressway
Brownsville, TX 78521
512–544–2323

115. Eugene, OR

KCBY–TV (CBS)
611 Coalbank Slough Rd.
Coos Bay, OR 97420
503–269–1111

KEZI (ABC)
2225 Coburg Rd.
Eugene, OR 97401
503–485–5611

KMTR–TV (NBC)
3825 International Ct.
Springfield, OR 97477
503–746–1600

KVAL–TV (CBS)
Box 1313
Eugene, OR 97440
503–342–4961

116. Tallahassee, FL

WCTV (CBS)
Box 3048
Tallahassee, FL 32315
904–893–6666

WTWC (NBC)
8440 Deerlake Rd.
Tallahassee, FL 32312
904–893–4140

WTXL–TV (ABC)
8927 Thomasville Rd.
Tallahassee, FL 32312
904–893–3127

117. Reno, NV

KOLO–TV (ABC)
4850 Ampere Dr.
Reno, NV 89502
702–786–8880

KRNV (NBC)
1790 Vassar St.
Reno, NV 89510
702–322–4444

KTVN (CBS)
4925 Energy Way
Reno, NV 89502
702–862–2212

118. Lafayette, LA

KADN (Fox, ABC)
1500 Eraste Landry Rd.
Lafayette, LA 70506
318–237–1500

KATC (ABC)
Box 93133
Lafayette, LA 70509
318–235–3333

KLFY–TV (CBS)
Box 90665
Lafayette, LA 70509
318–981–4823

119. Fort Smith, AR

KHOG–TV (ABC)
15 N. Church St.
Fayetteville, AR 72702
501–521–1010

KFSM–TV (CBS)
Box 369
Fort Smith, AR 72902
501–783–3131

KHBS (ABC)
2415 N. Albert Pike
Fort Smith, AR 72904
501–783–4040

KPOM–TV (NBC)
Box 4610
Fort Smith, AR 72914
501–785–2400

120. Macon, GA

WGXA (ABC)
Box 340
Macon, GA 31297
912–745–2424

WMAZ–TV (CBS)
Box 5008
Macon, GA 31213
912–752–1313

WMGT (NBC)
6525 Ocmulgee E. Blvd.
Macon, GA 31213
912–745–4141

121. Tyler, TX

KETK–TV (NBC)
4300 Richmond Rd.
Tyler, TX 75703
903–581–5656

KLTV (ABC)
2609 E. Irwin
Tyler, TX 75702
903–597–5588

KTRE–TV (CBS)
Box 729
Lufkin, TX 75901
409–853–5873

122. Traverse City–Cadillac, MI

WWTV (CBS)
10360 N. 130th Ave.
Cadillac, MI 49601
616–775–3478

WPBN–TV (NBC)
Box 546
Traverse City, MI 49684
616–947–7770

WGTU (ABC)
201 E. Front St.
Traverse City, MI 49684
616–946–2900

WWUP–TV (CBS)
601 Osborne
Sault Ste. Marie, MI 49783
906–635–6225

123. Columbus, GA

WLTZ (NBC)
6140 Buena Vista Rd.
Columbus, GA 31995
404–561–3838

WRBL (CBS)
1350 13th Ave.
Columbus, GA 31994
404–323–3333

WTVM (ABC)
Box 1848
Columbus, GA 31902
404–324–6471

124. Yakima–Pasco–Richland–Kennewick, WA

KEPR–TV (CBS)
2807 W. Lewis
Pasco, WA 99301
509–547–0547

KNDU (NBC)
3312 W. Kennewick Ave.
Kennewick, WA 99336
509–783–6151

KAPP (ABC)
1610 S. 24th Ave.
Yakima, WA 98902
509–453–0351

KIMA–TV (CBS)
2801 Terrace Heights Dr.
Yakima, WA 98901
509–575–0029

KNDO (NBC)
1608 S. 24th Ave.
Yakima, WA 98902
509–248–2300

KVEW
601 N. Edison
Kennewick, WA 99336
509–735–8369

125. Chico–Redding, CA

KCPM (NBC)
180 E. Fourth St.
Chico, CA 95928
916–893–2424

KHSL–TV (CBS)
Box 489
Chico, CA 95927
916–342–0141

KRCR–TV (ABC)
755 Auditorium Dr.
Redding, CA 96001
510–768–6731

126. Bakersfield, CA

KBAK–TV (ABC)
Box 2929
Bakersfield, CA 93303
805–327–7955

KERO–TV (CBS)
321 21st St.
Bakersfield, CA 93301
805–327–1441

KGET (NBC)
2831 Eye St.
Bakersfield, CA 93301
805–327–7511

127. Duluth–Superior, MN

KBJR–TV (NBC)
230 E. Superior St.
Duluth, MN 55802
218–727–8484

KDLH (CBS)
425 W. Superior St.
Duluth, MN 55802
218–727–8911

WDIO–TV (ABC)
10 Observation Rd.
Duluth, MN 55816
218–727–6864

128. Amarillo, TX

KAMR–TV (NBC)
Box 751
Amarillo, TX 79189
806–383–3321

KFDA–TV (CBS)
Broadway & Cherry
Amarillo, TX 79189
806–383–2226

KVII–TV (ABC)
One Broadcast Ctr.
Amarillo, TX 79101
806–373–1787

**129. Monroe, LA–
El Dorado, AR**

KNOE–TV (CBS)
Box 4067
Monroe, LA 71211
318–388–8888

KARD (ABC)
102 Thomas Rd., Ste. 22
W. Monroe, LA 71291
318–323–1972

KTVE (NBC)
400 W. Main
El Dorado, AR 71730
501–862–6651

**130. Florence–
Myrtle Beach, SC**

WBTW (CBS)
3430 TV Rd.
Florence, SC 29501
803–662–1565

WPDE–TV (ABC)
Box F–15
Florence, SC 29501
803–665–1515

WGSE
Box 1243
Myrtle Beach, SC 29577
803–626–4300

131. Corpus Christi, TX

KEDT (noncommercial)
4455 W. Padre Island Dr.
Corpus Christi, TX 78411
512–855–2213

KIII (ABC)
Box 6669
Corpus Christi, TX 78411
512–854–4733

KORO (Univision)
102 N. Mesquite
Corpus Christi, TX 78403
512–883–2823

KRIS–TV (NBC, Fox)
409 S. Staples St.
Corpus Christi, TX 78401
512–883–6100

KZTV (CBS)
301 Artesian
Corpus Christi, TX 78403
512–883–7070

132. Wausau–Rhinelander, WI

WJFW–TV (NBC)
South Ondda Ave.
Rhinelander, WI 54501
715–369–4700

WAOW–TV (ABC)
1908 Grand Ave.
Wausau, WI 54401
715–842–2251

WSAW–TV (CBS)
1114 Grand Ave.
Wausau, WI 54401
715–845–4211

133. Columbus–Tupelo–West Point, MS

WCBI–TV (CBS)
Box 271
Columbus, MS 39703
601–327–4444

WTVA (NBC)
Box 350
Tupelo, MS 39773
601–842–7620

WLOV–TV (ABC)
Box 777
West Point, MS 39773
601–494–8327

134. La Crosse–Eau Claire, WI

WEAU–TV (NBC)
1907 S. Hastings Way
Eau Claire, WI 54702
715–835–1313

WQOW–TV (ABC)
2881 S. Hastings Way
Eau Claire, WI 54701
715–835–1881

WKBT (CBS)
141 S. Sixth St.
La Crosse, WI 54601
608–782–4678

WXOW–TV
3705 County Hwy. 25
La Crescent, MN 55947
507–895–9969

135. Boise, ID

KAID (noncommercial)
1910 University Dr.
Boise, ID 83725
208–385–3727

KBCI–TV (CBS)
1007 W. Jefferson
Boise, ID 83707
208–336–5222

KIVI (ABC)
1866 E. Chisholm Dr.
Nampa, ID 83687
208–336–0500

KTVB (NBC)
Box 7
Boise, ID 83707
208–375–7277

KTRV (Fox)
679 Sixth St. N. Ext.
Nampa, ID 83652
208–466–1200

136. Wheeling, WV–Steubenville, OH

WTRF–TV (CBS, ABC)
96 16th St.
Wheeling, WV 26003
304–232–7777

WTOV–TV (NBC)
Altamont Hill
Steubenville, OH 43952
614–282–0911

137. Beaumont–Port Arthur, TX

KBMT (ABC)
525 I–10 South
Beaumont, TX 77701
409–833–7512

KFDM–TV (CBS)
Box 7128
Beaumont, TX 77726
409–892–6622

KJAC–TV (NBC)
2900 17th St.
Beaumont, TX 77642
409–985–5557

138. Rockford, IL

WIFR–TV (CBS)
2523 N. Meridian Rd.
Rockford, IL 61103
815–987–5300

WREX–TV (ABC)
10322 W. Auburn Rd.
Rockford, IL 61103
815–968–1813

WTVO (NBC)
1917 N. Meridian Rd.
Rockford, IL 61105
815–963–5413

139. Topeka, KS

KSNT (NBC)
Box 2700
Topeka, KS 66601
913–582–4000

KTKA–TV (ABC)
101 S.E. Monroe
Topeka, KS 66603
913–234–4949

WIBW–TV (CBS)
5600 W. Sixth St.
Topeka, KS 66606
913–272–3456

140. Wichita Falls, TX–Lawton, OK

KSWO–TV (ABC)
Box 708, Highway 7
Lawton, OK 73502
405–355–7000

KAUZ–TV (CBS)
Box 2130
Wichita Falls, TX 76307
817–322–6957

KFDX–TV (NBC)
4500 Seymour Hwy.
Wichita Falls, TX 76309
817–692–4530

141. Erie, PA

WICU–TV (NBC)
3514 State St.
Erie, PA 16508
814–454–5201

WJET–TV (ABC)
8455 Peach St.
Erie, PA 16509
814–864–2400

WSEE–TV (CBS)
1220 Peach St.
Erie, PA 16501
814–455–7575

142. Sioux City, IA

KCAU–TV (ABC)
Seventh & Douglas St.
Sioux City, IA 51101
712–277–2345

KMEG (CBS)
Box 657
Sioux City, IA 51102
712–277–3554

KTIV (NBC)
3135 Floyd Blvd.
Sioux City, IA 51105
712–239–4100

143. Terre Haute, IN

WBAK–TV (ABC)
Box 719
Terre Haute, IN 47808
812–238–1515

WTHI–TV (CBS)
918 Ohio St.
Terre Haute, IN 47808
812–232–9481

WTWO (NBC)
Box 299
Terre Haute, IN 47808
812–696–2121

144. Wilmington, NC

WECT (NBC)
Box 4029
Wilmington, NC 28406
919–791–8070

WJKA (CBS)
1926 Oleander Dr.
Wilmington, NC 28403
919–343–8826

WWAY (ABC)
Box 2068
Wilmington, NC 28402
919–762–8581

145. Rochester, MN– Mason City, IA–Austin, MN

KAAL (ABC)
Box 577
Austin, MN 55912
507–433–8836

KIMT (CBS)
112 N. Pennsylvania Ave.
Mason City, IA 50401
515–423–2540

KTTC (NBC)
601 First Ave. SW
Rochester, MN 55902
507–288–4444

146. Medford, OR

KDRV (ABC)
1090 Knutson Ave.
Medford, OR 97504
503–773–1212

KOBI (NBC)
125 S. Fir St.
Medford, OR 97501
503–779–5555

KTVL (CBS)
1440 Rossanley Dr.
Medford, OR 97501
503–773–7373

147. Joplin, MO–Pittsburg, KS

KODE–TV (ABC)
1928 W. 13th St.
Joplin, MO 64801
417–623–7260

KSNF–TV (NBC)
Box 1393
Joplin, MO 64802
417–781–2345

KOAM–TV (CBS)
Highway 69 & Lawton Rd.
Pittsburg, KS 66762
417–624–0233

148. Binghamton, NY

WBNG–TV (CBS)
50 Front St.
Binghamton, NY 13902
607–723–7311

WICZ–TV (NBC)
4600 Vestal Pkwy. E.
Vestal, NY 13850
607–770–4040

WMGC–TV (ABC)
Ingraham Hill Rd.
Binghamton, NY 13902
607–723–7464

WSKG (noncommercial)
Willow Point Broadcast Ctr.
Binghamton, NY 13902
607–729–4100

149. Lubbock, TX

KAMC (ABC)
1201 84th St.
Lubbock, TX 79423
806–745–2828

KCBD–TV (NBC)
Box 2190
Lubbock, TX 79408
806–744–1414

KLBK–TV (CBS)
7400 S. University Ave.
Lubbock, TX 79408
806–745–2345

150. Columbia–Jefferson City, MO

KMIZ (ABC)
501 Business Loop 70 East
Columbia, MO 65201
314–449–0917

KOMU–TV (NBC)
Highway 63 S.
Columbia, MO 65201
314–442–1122

KRCG (CBS)
Old Highway 54
Holts Summit, MO 65043
314–896–5144

151. Bluefield–Beckley–Oak Hill, WV

WVVA (NBC)
Route 460 Bypass
Bluefield, WV 24701
304–325–5487

WOAY–TV (ABC)
Box 251
Oak Hill, WV 25901
304–469–3361

152. Odessa–Midland, TX

KMID–TV (ABC)
3200 Laforce Blvd.
Midland, TX 79711
915–563–2222

KOSA–TV (CBS)
1211 N. Whitaker St.
Odessa, TX 79763
915–337–8301

KTPX (NBC)
Box 60150
Midland, TX 79711
915–563–4210

**153. Minot–Bismarck–
Dickinson, ND**

KFYR–TV (NBC)
200 N. Fourth St.
Bismarck, ND 58501
701–255–5757

KXMB–TV (CBS)
1811 N. 15th St.
Bismarck, ND 53501
701–223–9197

KMCY (ABC)
Box 2276
Minot, ND 58702
701–838–6614

KMOT (NBC)
1800 S.W. 16th St.
Minot, ND 58702
701–852–4101

KXMC–TV (CBS)
Box 1686
Minot, ND 58701
701–852–2104

154. Albany, GA

WALB–TV (NBC)
1709 Stuart Ave.
Albany, GA 31708
912–883–0154

WFXL (Fox)
Box 4050
Albany, GA 31708
912–435–3100

WVGA (ABC)
275 Norman Dr.
Valdosta, GA 31603
912–242–4444

155. Bangor, ME

WABI–TV (CBS)
35 Hildreth St.
Bangor, ME 04401
207–947–8321

WLBZ–TV (NBC)
Mt. Hope Ave.
Bangor, ME 04401
207–942–4822

WVII–TV (ABC)
371 Target Industrial Cir.
Bangor, ME 04401
207–945–6457

WMEB–TV (noncommercial)
65 Texas Ave.
Bangor, ME 04401
207–941–1010

156. Palm Springs, CA

KESQ–TV (ABC)
42–650 Melanie Pl.
Palm Desert, CA 92260
619–773–0342

KMIR–TV (NBC)
72920 Parkview Dr.
Palm Desert, CA 92260
619–568–3636

157. Anchorage, AK

KIMO (ABC)
2700 E. Tudor Rd.
Anchorage, AK 99507
907–561–1313

KTUU–TV (NBC)
Box 102880
Anchorage, AK 99510
907–257–0202

KTVA (CBS)
1007 West 32nd Ave.
Anchorage, AK 99503
907–562–3456

158. Quincy, IL–Hannibal, MO

KHQA–TV (CBS)
510 Main St.
Quincy, IL 62301
217–222–6200

WGEM–TV (NBC)
513 Hampshire St.
Quincy, IL 62306
217–228–6600

WTJR
Old Cannonball Rd.
Quincy, IL 62305
217–228–1275

159. Abilene–Sweetwater, TX

KRBC–TV (NBC)
Box 178
Abilene, TX 79604
915–692–4242

KTAB–TV (CBS)
5401 S. 14th St.
Abilene, TX 79608
915–695–2777

KTXS–TV (ABC)
Box 2997
Abilene, Texas 79604
915–677–2281

160. Biloxi–Gulfport, MS

WLOX–TV (ABC)
208 De Buys Rd.
Biloxi, MS 39535
601–896–1313

161. Clarksburg–Weston, WV

WBO–TV (NBC)
912 West Pike St.
Clarksburg, WV 26302
304–623–3311

WDTV (CBS)
5 Television Dr.
Bridgeport, WV 26330
304–623–5555

162. Idaho Falls–Pocatello, ID

KIDK (CBS)
1255 E. 17th St.
Idaho Falls, ID 83404
208–522–5100

KIFI–TV (NBC)
1915 N. Yellowstone Hwy.
Idaho Falls, ID 83401
208–525–8888

KPVI (ABC)
Box 667
Pocatello, ID 83204
208–232–6666

KISU–TV (noncommercial)
Box 8111/Idaho State Univ.
Pocatello, ID 83209
208–236–2857

163. Utica, NY

WKTV (NBC)
Box 2
Utica, NY 13503
315–733–0404

WUTR (ABC)
Box 20
Utica, NY 13503
315–797–5220

164. Dothan, AL

WDHN (ABC)
Highway 52 East
Dothan, AL 36302
205–793–1818

WTVY (CBS)
Box 1089
Dothan, AL 36301
205–792–3195

165. Salisbury, MD

WBOC–TV (CBS)
Radio TV Pk.
Salisbury, MD 21801
301–749–1111

WMDI (ABC–NBC)
202 Downtown Plaza
Salisbury, MD 21801
301–742–4747

166. Elmira, NY

WENY–TV (ABC)
Box 208
Elmira, NY 14902
607–739–3636

WETM–TV (NBC)
One Broadcast Ctr.
Elmira, NY 14901
607–733–5518

167. Gainesville, FL

WCJB–TV (ABC)
6220 N.W. 43rd St.
Gainesville, FL 32614
904–377–2020

**168. Laurel–
Hattiesburg, MS**

WDAM–TV (NBC)
Box 16269
Hattiesburg, MS 39402
601–544–4730

WHLT (CBS)
990 Hardy St.
Hattiesburg, MS 39401
601–545–2077

169. Panama City, FL

WJHG–TV (NBC)
8195 Front Beach Rd.
Panama City Beach, FL 32413
904–234–2125

WMBB (ABC)
613 Harrison Ave.
Panama City, FL 32402
904–769–2313

WPGX (Fox)
700 W. 23rd St., Ste. 28
Panama City, FL 32405
904–784–0028

170. Alexandria, LA

KALB–TV (NBC)
605–11 Washington St.
Alexandria, LA 71301
318–445–2456

KLAX–TV (ABC)
1811 England Dr.
Alexandria, LA 71306
318–473–0031

171. Billings–Hardin, MT

KTVQ (CBS)
Box 2557
Billings, MT 59103
406–252–5611

KULR–TV (NBC)
2045 Overland Ave.
Billings, MT 59102
406–656–8000

KOUS–TV (ABC)
445 S. 24th St., W.
Billings, MT 59104
406–652–4743

172. Rapid City, SD

KCLO–TV (CBS)
2497 W. Chicago St.
Rapid City, SD 57702
605–341–1500

KEVN–TV (NBC)
Box 677
Rapid City, SD 57709
605–394–7776

KOTA (ABC)
Box 1760
Rapid City, SD 57709
605–342–2000

173. Greenwood–Greenville, MS

WABG–TV (ABC)
849 Washington Ave.
Greenville, MS 38701
601–332–0949

WXVT (CBS)
3015 E. Reed Rd.
Greenville, MS 38703
601–334–1500

174. Watertown, NY

WNPE–TV (noncommercial)
Arsenal St.
Watertown, NY 13601
315–782–3142

WWNY–TV (CBS, NBC)
120 Arcade St.
Watertown, NY 13601
315–788–3800

WWTI (ABC)
Box 6250
Watertown, NY 13601
315–785–8850

175. Jonesboro, AR

KAIT–TV (ABC)
Highway 41 N.
Jonesboro, AR 72401
501–931–8888

176. Lake Charles, LA

KPLC–TV (NBC)
320 Division St.
Lake Charles, LA 70601
318–439–9071

KVHP (Fox)
129 W. Prien Lake Rd.
Lake Charles, LA 70602
318–474–1316

177. Missoula, MT

KECI–TV (NBC)
340 W. Main
Missoula, MT 59802
406–721–2063

KPAX–TV (CBS)
2204 Regent St.
Missoula, MT 59801
406–543–7106

178. El Centro, CA–Yuma, AZ

KECY–TV (CBS)
646 Main St.
El Centro, CA 92243
619–353–9990

KSWT (ABC)
1301 Third Ave.
Yuma, AZ 85364
602–782–5113

KYMA (ABC)
1385 S. Pacific Ave.
Yuma, AZ 85365
602–782–1111

179. Ardmore–Ada, OK

KTEN (ABC, NBC)
101 E. Main
Denison, TX 75020
214–465–5836

KXII (CBS, NBC)
4201 Texoma Pkwy.
Sherrnan, TX 75090
903–892–8123

180. Marquette, MI

WLUC–TV (CBS, NBC)
177 U.S. Highway 41
Negaunee, MI 49866
906–475–4161

181. Meridian, MS

WTOK–TV (ABC)
Box 2988
Meridian, MS 39302
601–693–1441

WTZH (CBS)
Box 5185
Meridian, MS 39301
601–693–2933

182. Great Falls, MT

KFBB–TV (ABC)
Havre Hwy.
Great Falls, MT 59403
406–453–4377

KRTV (CBS)
Box 1331
Great Falls, MT 59403
406–453–2431

KTGF (NBC)
118 Sixth St. South
Great Falls, MT 59405
406–761–8816

183. Parkersburg, WV

WTAP–TV (NBC)
One Television Plaza
Parkersburg, WV 26101
304–485–4588

184. St. Joseph, MO

KQTV (ABC)
40th & Faron Sts.
St. Joseph, MO 64506
816–364–2222

185. Jackson, TN

WBBJ–TV (ABC)
346 Muse St.
Jackson, TN 38301
901–424–4515

186. Mankato, MN

KEYC–TV (CBS)
1570 Lookout Dr.
N. Mankato, MN 56001
507–625–7905

187. Tuscaloosa, AL

WCFT–TV (CBS)
4000 37th St. East
Tuscaloosa, AL 35405
205–553–1333

188. Eureka, CA

KIEM–TV (NBC)
5650 S. Broadway
Eureka, CA 95501
707–443–3123

KVIQ (CBS)
1800 Broadway
Eureka, CA 95501
707–443–3061

189. Grand Junction–Durango, CO

KJCT (ABC)
Box 3788
Grand Junction, CO 81502
303–245–8880

KREX–TV (CBS)
Box 789
Grand Junction, CO 81502
303–242–5000

190. Bowling Green, KY

WBKO (ABC)
2727 Russellville Rd.
Bowling Green, KY 42101
502–781–1313

191. Butte, MT

KTVM (NBC)
750 Dewey Blvd., Ste. 1
Butte, MT 59701
406–494–7603

KXLF–TV (CBS)
1003 S. Montana
Butte, MT 59701
406–782–0444

192. San Angelo, TX

KLST (CBS)
2800 Armstrong
San Angelo, TX 76903
915–949–8800

193. Lafayette, IN

WLFI–TV (CBS)
2605 Yeager Rd.
West Lafayette, IN 47906
317–463–1800

194. Casper–Riverton, WY

KGWC–TV (CBS, Fox)
304 N. Center
Casper, WY 82601
307–234–1111

KTWO–TV (NBC)
4200 E. Second St.
Casper, WY 82602
307–237–3711

KFNE (ABC, CBS)
7075 Salt Creek Rd.
Casper, WY 82601
307–237–2020

KGWR–TV (CBS)
Box 170
Casper, WY 82602
307–234–1111

195. Charlottesville, VA

WVIR–TV (NBC)
503 E. Market St.
Charlottesville, VA 22902
804–977–7082

196. Anniston, AL

WJSU–TV (CBS)
1330 Noble St.
Anniston, AL 36202
205–237–8651

197. Cheyenne, WY-Scottsbluff, NE

KGWN–TV (CBS, ABC)
2923 E. Lincolnway
Cheyenne, WY 82001
307–634–7755

KKTU (NBC)
4200 E. Second St.
Cheyenne, WY 82069
307–237–3711

KDUH–TV (ABC)
Box 1529
Scottsbluff, NE 69363
308–632–3071

KSTF (CBS, Fox)
3385 N. Tenth Ave.
Gering, NE 69341
308–632–6107

198. Ottumwa, IA-Kirksville, MO

KOIA–TV (Fox)
820 W. Second St.
Ottumwa, IA 52501
515–684–5415

KTVO (ABC)
Box 949
Kirksville, MO 63501
816–627–3333

199. Lima, OH

WLIO (NBC)
1424 Rice Ave.
Lima, OH 48505
419–228–8835

200. Laredo, TX

KGNS–TV (NBC)
102 W. Del Mar Blvd.
Laredo, TX 78044
512–727–8888

201. Harrisonburg, VA

WHSV–TV (ABC)
Highway 33 West
Harrisonburg, VA 22801
703–433–9191

202. Zanesville, OH

WHIZ–TV (NBC)
629 Downard Rd.
Zanesville, OH 43701
614–452–5431

203. Twin Falls, ID

KMVT (CBS)
1100 Blue Lakes Blvd., N.
Twin Falls, ID 83301
208–733–1100

204. Presque Isle, ME

WAGM–TV (CBS, ABC, NBC)
Box 1149
Presque Isle, ME 04769
207–764–4461

205. Bend, OR

KTVZ (NBC)
62990 O.B. Riley Rd.
Bend, OR 97701
503–383–2121

206. Fairbanks, AK

KATN (ABC, NBC)
Box 74730
Fairbanks, AK 99707
907–452–2125

KTVF (CBS, NBC)
3528 International
Fairbanks, AK 99701
907–452–5121

207. Victoria, TX

KAVU–TV (ABC, NBC)
3808 N. Navarro
Victoria, TX 77903
512–575–2500

208. Helena, MT

KTVH (NBC)
2433 N. Montana Ave.
Helena, MT 59601
406–443–5050

209. Alpena, MI

WBKB–TV (CBS)
1390 Bagley St.
Alpena, MI 49707
517–356–3434

210. North Platte, NE

KNOP–TV (NBC)
Box 749
North Platte, NE 69103
308–532–2222

KPNE–TV (PBS)
Box 83111
Lincoln, NE 68501
402–472–3611

211. Glendive, MT

KXGN–TV (CBS)
201 S. Douglas St.
Glendive, MT 59330
406–365–3377

Glossary

A-roll: Videotape containing major elements to be included in the edit of a package. *See B-roll.*

ADI: Area of dominant influence. Designation for a geographical area as measured by Arbitron.

ADO: Ampex Digital Optics. A digital-effects device.

AEJMC: Association for Education in Journalism and Mass Communication.

affiliate: Television station aligned with a network to broadcast network programs.

AFTRA: American Federation of Television and Radio Artists. A union.

aspect ratio: The proportional dimensions of the television screen, which measures three units high and four units wide.

ATC: Audiotape cartridge (or cart). In news operations, audiotape is stored on a continuous-loop cart that starts and stops instantly.

B-roll: Additional videotape footage, such as cutaways, cut-ins, and reaction shots used to create continuity. *See A-roll.*

backtiming: The act of determining the amount of time left in a program by subtracting the present program time from the total program time.

beeper: A phone call on the air.

Betacam: A component direct-color broadcast-quality 1/2-inch format developed by Sony; the current industry standard.

Betamax: The first successful consumer VCR tape format, invented by Sony in 1975; now extinct and not to be confused with 1/2-inch professional Betacam and Betacam SP tape formats.

burn-in time code: Hours, minutes, seconds, and frames that have been inserted into the video by a character generator.

bust shot: A camera shot that shows the person from the chest up.

C-band: Most widely used band of frequencies for satellite transmission and reception.

camcorder: A video-acquisition device that combines a camera and a VCR into a single portable unit.

cardioid: A microphone with a heart-shaped pickup pattern.

CATV: Community antenna television. Generic term for all cable television in the 1950s and 1960s. Also a cable system's delivery to homes of programs picked up directly off the air as opposed to importation.

chromakey: A method of shooting an object or a person against a green or blue background; the colored background is then electronically replaced by another video signal. *See Ultimatte.*

chrominance: The color portion of a composite video signal.

Chyron: The trade name of the video word processor, or character generator, that creates letters and other graphic elements.

clear-clutch: A page of black that must occur between a full-screen insertion from the still-store and an over-the-shoulder insertion from the still-store.

component: A video signal in which the luminance and chrominance are handled on separate and alternate tracks of the videotape.

composite: The full video signal, including colorburst, synch, and picture information.

control room: Location where the newscast is electronically produced and assembled.

copy: Anything written for broadcast.

cue: Anything that calls for a change in the audio or video.

cut: Replacing one video source with another; often referred to as a take.

cutaway shot: A shot that draws attention away from the main subject, usually of short duration, and often used as a cover for an edit point.

D-1, D-2, D-3, D-5: Digital tape formats. The Japanese symbol for D-4 means "death" and is not used.

DBS: Direct broadcast satellite. The transmission of TV programs to the home from satellites 23,000 miles above the earth, using a 120-watt signal received by an 18-inch dish.

debrief: When an anchor interviews a reporter or expert about a story or issue.

demographics: Breaking down a viewing audience by various social and economic characteristics, such as age, sex, income, and education. Also referred to as demos.

dissolve: Replacing one video source with another by fading out on one and fading in on the other.

DMA: Designated market area. Geographic area as measured by Nielsen Media Research.

double box: An electronic effect that puts two video sources side by side on the screen.

downlink: The process in which a satellite transforms a signal's frequency and retransmits it to stations on the ground.

dub: Copying an audio or video signal from one tape to another.

EFP: Electronic field production. The use of single-camera, film-style techniques to acquire images and sound. It is distinguished from ENG by the amount of time available to set the lighting and gather information.

EFX: Effects.

ENG: Electronic newsgathering. The process of employing a battery-powered camcorder to acquire images and audio for news production.

fade: A transition from the video source to black or vice versa.

Fairness Doctrine: FCC rules and policies requiring stations to devote a reasonable amount of time to discussion of controversial issues and to see that opposing points of view are aired.

feed: Any electronic signal that travels from source to receiver.

fiber optics: Distribution of television material, imposed on light waves, through a hair-thin glass core. The light waves can be modulated and sent across great distances, with improved opportunity for multiplexing.

floor manager: Individual responsible for all activities on the studio floor and for relaying the newscast director's signals to the talent during rehearsal and production. Also called stage manager.

future file: Story ideas to be worked on in the near future.

generic live shot: A live shot that begins at a set time (usually at 6:01 or 11:01 p.m.) from some major national story; it is then carried simultaneously by many local newscasts across the time zone. All four news networks provide these for affiliates.

genlock: A system that uses synch from a video source and locks onto an incoming signal.

geosynchronous satellite: A transponding device that orbits 22,300 miles above the earth at the same speed as the rotation of the earth. This allows it to appear stationary over the ground station it is communicating with, so it acts much like a broadcasting tower.

group owner: Single licensee of stations in two or more communities.

happy talk: A style of casual conversation among anchors to take the edge off hard news.

hard news: News with immediacy, timeliness, and directness; as opposed to the human-interest story.

HDTV: High-definition television. A television receiver with more than twice the scan lines as NTSC consumer television, with an aspect ratio of 16:9.

headend: The system site of a CATV operation that receives programs from a variety of sources.

hertz: One cycle per second (frequency with which wave crests pass a given point). The abbreviations *kHz* and *mHz* refer to thousands and millions of cycles per second, respectively.

HFR: Hold for release. Stories shot one day and aired later.

Hi-8: A high-quality 8mm videotape format introduced by Sony in 1989 with performance specs similar to Super VHS.

It is ideal as an acquisition format because of its extreme portability.

hot-switching: Slang term for live-switching among multiple cameras.

IATSE: International Alliance of Theatrical Stage Employees. A union.

IBEW: International Brotherhood of Electrical Workers. A union.

IFB: Interruptible fold-back. Also known as interrupted feed-back. An earpiece worn by talent that carries the program sound or information from the newscast director.

independent station: A station having no relationship with a network.

insert edit: Electronic videotape editing in which new video, audio, or both can be inserted into a previously recorded tape without disturbing material before and after the insert. Insert editing utilizes the existing control track and produces very stable edits.

interactive capacity: The ability of a cable system to carry signals from a subscribing home back to the headend.

ITVA: International Television and Video Association.

kicker: The last newscast segment or story that airs before end credits during a broadcast.

KU-band: That band of frequencies located above C-band, used for satellite transmission and reception.

lead-in audience: The portion of the audience viewing the preceding program that remains for the next program.

live feed: Transmission to the broadcast studio from an external source taking place in real time.

live wraparound: Reporter doing a live report before and after a taped package on the same subject.

local slant: Reworking a national or international story to show relevance to a station's own DMA.

luminance: The brightness of the video image; symbolized by the letter Y.

lux: The amount of light present one meter away from a source of one candlepower.

M-II: Component direct-color 1/2-inch tape format developed by JVC and Panasonic.

master control: The final destination for all processed information prior to sending the signal to the transmitter.

microwave: Line-of-sight electronic transmission of high-frequency RF energy between fixed points, usually viable up to fifty miles.

microwave relay: Distribution of television and other signals by beamed radio relay between high buildings or mountains.

mix-minus: A signal provided to the talent that allows them to hear all other audio except their own voice.

MTS: Multichannel television sound. Hi-fi stereo sound on television programs.

narrowcasting: The programming philosophy that provides specific program content to a targeted demographic. MTV or ESPN are primary examples.

nat sound: Natural sound. The ambient sound from the scene of a story not covered by track or narration.

network: A number of stations making an arrangement with an organization to carry programming distributed by that organization. The major networks in the United States are ABC, CBS, NBC, and Fox. The beginning of the 1980s saw the formation of satellite-based cable networks such as CNN, Discovery, MTV, and USA.

O&O: A television station that is owned and operated by a network.

OTS: Over-the-shoulder shot.

outcue: The last words or images in the video or audio that the newscast director may use to time a transition.

outtakes: Any picture and sound materials that have been edited out of the package ultimately broadcast.

package: A story edited and assembled and rolled into the newscast as a self-contained unit.

promo: Anything that airs which teases or attracts viewer attention to the station's own programming.

PSA: Public service announcement. Time donated by a station to fulfill its obligations to the community.

quad: Quadraplex. The original videotape two-inch format using four video heads and a segmented recording system. Once dominant in broadcast TV, it is now found only in the smallest markets.

the quad: Slang for the tape room at WJZ-TV

reaction shot: Footage necessary to show a person's response to someone.

remote: Any broadcast sent back live to the newsroom from a location outside the station.

remote unit: The equipment required to originate a television program from a location outside the studio.

rip-and-read: Copy that comes directly from a major wire service and is read on-air without editing or rewriting.

robotic camera: A studio camera that incorporates a remotely controlled pan and tilt head, and a free-roaming pedestal.

router: A routing switcher. A device that dispatches video signals to a variety of audio or video equipment.

RTNDA: Radio and Television News Directors Association.

rundown: A log for the technical crew containing precisely timed stories in the sequence they will be broadcast.

SAG: Screen Actors Guild. A union.

script: A precise, sequential copy of each story in the show, the text of which is carried and displayed on the TelePrompTer.

shot: A continuous run of the camcorder at a given scene.

sidebar: Story that explains an issue related to a main part of the story.

slug: An identifier to cue recognition of a particular story usually found on the rundown or script pages.

SMPTE: Society of Motion Picture and Television Engineers.

soft news: Features and stories that can be used over time without a loss of news value; these usually involve local color and human interest.

SOT: Sound-on-tape.

sound bite: An audio clip of dialogue or ambient sound necessary to enhance the telling of a story.

soundtrack: Narration for a video piece.

spot: Commercial to be automatically inserted by computer into the newscast.

still-store: Still-frame storage unit. A computerized digital library device that stores individual video frames as digital information. The frames can be recalled by addressing their location in the computer. This device made obsolete the slide chain and camera card processes.

super: A special kind of dissolve, in which two images appear on screen simultaneously.

Super VHS: 1/2-inch videotape format introduced by JVC in 1987 that significantly improves the VHS format by changing the way the luminance component of the video is processed and recorded.

Super VHS-C: 1/2-inch videotape format using cassettes similar in size to that of Hi-8; maximizes portability and convenience.

superstation: A television station carried by local cable companies around the country via geosynchronous satellite. Also known as a satellite-based network, WTBS and WOR are prime examples.

sweep: A period during which television audiences are intensely measured.

switcher: Electronic device used to select among numerous video sources for either broadcast or recording. Also, the production crew member who operates the video switcher (or the technical director).

synch: Synchronization. A pulse that controls timing.

syndication: Sale of program material directly to stations.

tag: The last words of a story.

take: To cut to a video source. Usually a director's command, as in "Take 1." Also, individual scenes, segments, or shots recorded on film or videotape. Each is assigned a "take number," which is used to locate and identify the segments for screening and editing.

talent: Anyone who is in front of the camera.

talkback: Q&A with an expert or public figure, often live.

talking head: A sound bite with the video of the person speaking.

TBC: Time-base corrector. A device that corrects VCR stability errors during tape playback. Used with small-format VCRs such as the 3/4-inch U-matic.

tease: A short promotional clip that entices the viewer to watch a future story. Called a special tease by WJZ production team.

telecine: A combination film/slide projector and television camera used to convert film or stills into a television signal. Also known as a film chain.

transmitter: A broadcast device that modulates video onto an AM carrier wave and audio onto an FM carrier wave.

transponder: A device that combines the functions of transmitter and receiver, used in satellite communications.

U-matic: 3/4-inch videotape format developed by Sony in 1972; one of the first portable formats used for ENG.

UFVA: University Film and Video Association.

UHF: Ultra-high frequency television, channels 14 to 83.

Ultimatte: Trade name for the ultimate chromakey process that creates a technically superior broadcast image.

uplink: A ground station that sends a signal to a satellite.

upstream: The ability of the cable system to carry signals from a subscribing home back to the headend.

VCR: Videocassette recorder.

VHF: Very high frequency television, channels 2 to 13.

video compression: Digitizing a video image and encoding it in such a way that it can be stored and manipulated.

violator: The lower-third banners with Chyron text that have been keyed over a videotape.

V/O: Voiceover. Unseen speaker narrating accompanying video.

VTR: Video tape recorder.

wipe: A special-effects transition on the SEG that appears to move one image off the screen, replacing it with another.

wireless microphone: A microphone system that employs a radio transmitter and receiver.

wrap: The end. A signal that the newscast has finished.

zoom: A variable-focal-length lens; also a transition that artificially compresses space. This technique is overused in television and should be avoided whenever possible.

List of Works Cited

Adler, Dick. "News Meltdown Hits L.A." *Channels*, February 1987: 69–70.

Calem, Robert E. "TV News With a Bare-Bones Crew." *New York Times*, 23 May 1993: F9.

Celis, William, III. "New Tactics Urged to Raise Literacy." *The New York Times National*, 12 September 1993: 27.

Diamond, Edwin. "The Death of Truth." New York, 3 May 1993: 15.

Epstein, Edward Jay. *News from Nowhere*. New York: Random House, 1973.

Fuller, Harry. Personal correspondence. KPIX-TV, San Francisco. 29 August 1993.

Gross, Steve. "Hubbard's TV Venture via Satellite." *Minneapolis Star-Tribune*. Reprint made available by Hubbard Broadcasting.

Henry, William A., III. "News as Entertainment: The Search for Dramatic Unity." *What's News,* ed. Elie Abel. New York: Transaction Press, 1981.

Jorgensen, C. Peter. Memorandum. *Columbia Journalism Review*, January/February 1985: 18.

Kurtz, Howard. "Tabloid Sensationalism Is Thriving on TV News." *The Washington Post*, 4 July 1993: A20.

Mander, Jerry. *Four Arguments for the Elimination of Television.* New York: WilliamMorrow, 1978.

Minow, Newton N. Columbia University, Gannett Foundation Media Center, 9 May 1991.

Mitroff, Ian I., and Warren Bennis. *The Unreality Industry.* New York: Carol Publishing Group, 1993.

O'Donnell, Frank. "Confessions of a News Producer." *Regardie's,* February/March 1992: 37–41.

Parenti, Michael. *Inventing Reality.* New York: St. Martin's Press, 1993.

Rohter, Larry. "It Might Be News, But It's Not 'MacNeil/Lehrer.'" *New York Times,* 25 April 1993: H34.

Stephens, Mitchell. "The New TV: Stop Making Sense." *The Washington Post,* 25 April 1993: G5.

Stone, Vernon A. "Little Change for Minorities and Women." *Communicator,* August 1992: 26–27.

———. "New Salaries Stand Still." *Communicator,* February 1992: 14–15 .

Weaver, David H., and G. Cleveland Wilhoit. "The American Journalist in the 1990s." *Freedom Forum Report,* 17 November 1992.

Yoakam, Richard D., and Charles F. Cremer. *ENG: Television News and the New Technology.* New York: Random House, 1989.